YOU

THE individual You, your circumstances, your business and your leisure, your world in peace and war, you and love, you and death—these are some of the down-to-earth subjects which the author discusses in the light of Theosophy. Because of the clarity and enthusiasm with which he conveys his ideas, the book is an excellent introduction to Theosophy as a practical philosophy of life.

Dr. George S. Arundale was born and educated in England, where he joined The Theosophical Society and became one of its principal workers. He spent many years in India, where he was particularly active in the field of education. In 1934 he was elected the third international President of The Theosophical Society, an office he held until his death in 1945. He was the author of many works, including *Kundalini* and *The Lotus Fire*.

This popular book, now in a new edition, has introduced thousands of people to the value of Theosophy in meeting the problems of daily life.

I AM A KING

I who have seen the Heights and stood on their ascending,
Watching the shadows flee before the Day,
Know that our Lord the Sun is Life and Light unending,
Know that He moves resistless on His Way.

E'en in profoundest depths, where darkness seems eternal,
E'en where cold stillness spreads its blight afar,
There have I seen our Lord in all His Pow'r supernal,
There have I seen the Glory of His Star.

No storms of Life, nor griefs, shall drown me in disaster,
No hammer blows of Fate shall lay me low,
For I, though lone and weak, am, in His Light, their master.
E'en in the spark doth Fire of Sunlight glow.

I am the Light. No darkness can withstand my shining.
I am the Light—Ray of our Lord the Sun.
I am the Light—of every cloud the silver lining.
I am the Light—the many and the One.

So do I conquer depths of grim and dark descending,
So am I free—nor slave to weal or woe,
So do I conquer heights—for ever upward wending,
So am I King—to Dare, to Do, to Know.

YOU

BY

GEORGE S. ARUNDALE

A QUEST BOOK

Published under a grant from The Kern Foundation

THE THEOSOPHICAL PUBLISHING HOUSE

Wheaton, Ill., U.S.A.

Madras, India / London, England

First   edition   1935
Second printing   1936
Third   printing   1956

Quest Book Edition 1973 (slightly revised and
    abridged) published by The Theosophical
    Publishing House, Wheaton, Illinois, a
    department of The Theosophical Society
    in America, by arrangement with The
    Theosophical Publishing House, Madras

Arundale, George Sydney, 1878-1945.
  You.

  (A Quest book)
  1. Theosophy. I. Title.
BP565.A7Y62   192   73-4783
ISBN 0-8356-0434-9

FOREWORD

THIS book is a brief epitome of *my* Theosophy at its present stage of unfoldment, for though there are certain fundamental principles underlying the Science of Theosophy—possibly such as I have ventured to indicate in the Envoi—at the end, each student should be gradually finding his own Theosophy for himself, his own understanding of the science of living.

I have sketched mine in order that some of those who read this book may desire to find theirs—possibly, even probably, a Theosophy in many of its features radically different from my own. It must be clearly understood, therefore, that I am far from laying down the beliefs, opinions and principles current among Theosophists. Many may differ radically from me. So much the better. What each needs is his own, individually reached Theosophy, not somebody else's. My hope is that I have whetted the appetite of my readers for Theosophy, for the simple reason that I am so restlessly and discontentedly happy in mine, ever-changing as it fortunately is, ever growing, I hope, more closely resembling the Theosophy which is the eternal Science of Life.

G. S. A.

CONTENTS

INTRODUCTION

YOU IN GENERAL

A CONSIDERABLE proportion of the members of the human kingdom are probably sufficiently evolved to realize that the evolutionary process takes place under definite and immutable laws, and that it is directed to a definite goal.

Working inevitably in terms of very limited experience, we know little both as to the nature of these laws and as to the nature of the goal; and even the little we know is subject to that constant modification which growing knowledge insistently demands.

Theosophy is the Science of Life as so far discovered by those who are infinitely wiser than the wisest living in the outer world today. Their wisdom is reflected in the highest teaching given in religious philosophy and science, and has come down to us from those days, buried in the distant past, when the great standards for human development were both proclaimed and lived.

Ever since those days humanity has slowly, but surely, been growing in the direction of these standards, feeling its way towards them, building into the edifice of human consciousness brick upon brick of truth.

Theosophy is a statement of the Plan. Every human being is a builder learning to express the Plan in terms of his own individual life. At first he perceives but little of the Plan, and perceives that little inaccurately. He builds. He demolishes. But gradually a building rises which is according to Plan. When each individual building is complete, there will be no monotony of construction, so that the city presents an appearance of suburbia, for each abode will have its own distinctness, its own unique beauty—wondrous variations being rung on fundamental and eternal themes.

Throughout the world there are those who have come into contact with this Plan which is called Theosophy—the Divine Wisdom; and all who have grasped even the slightest fragment of it bear testimony to the fact that:

1. It offers the most intelligible and scientific explanation of Life as we know it in this outer world. It discloses cosmos where chaos seems to reign unchecked.

2. It sets forth in the most precise terms the origin, the way, and the goal of the Life we perceive to exist in ourselves and in all around us.

In this book the author tries to apply this Theosophy to the everyday affairs in the life of the everyday individual. But he wishes at the very outset to make clear that the Theosophy he thus seeks to apply is nothing more than Theosophy as, so far, he has been able to understand it. Who can know Theosophy in its ultimate conceptions save those who have learned all that life has to teach? Who shall dare to say: " This is Theosophy. There is no other! " ? A true student of Theosophy will say: " This is

Theosophy as I understand the science today. Tomorrow I hope to know more, and doubtless I shall tomorrow find much to modify in that which I know today."

The author, therefore, is offering the fruit of his studies as these have so far brought him. This book represents his untechnical interpretation of life resulting from a study of Theosophy for nearly thirty years. Other students may well have come to different conclusions. And the author himself may, if his book be still in demand some years hence, find occasion to modify much about which he feels reasonably sure today. But he thinks that the general principles will on the whole remain unchanged.

Deliberately, he has not ventured any description in detail of the teachings of Theosophy. Such description will be found in the literature of Theosophy, a list of which as suitable for further reading is given at the end. At the end also he summarizes what he believes to be the ultimate principles of Theosophy, while in this Chapter he sets forth certain general conceptions which may help to make clear his commentary on everyday life in terms of Theosophy.

But just as we are at first more concerned with the taste of a pudding than with its constituent elements, so let the reader see what Theosophy *does* to everyday life, how it explains our everyday surroundings and ourselves in the midst of them, how it tells us that life is supremely worth living, be circumstances what they may, how it insists upon the silver lining to every cloud however black, and upon the fact that someday there will be no clouds at all.

Our desire to know how the pudding is made will
be all the greater if we like the pudding. We shall be
more eager to know what is this Theosophy if we find
that it does things which make life easier and more
understandable.

In this book Theosophy is seen at work. If we like
the work we shall want to know more, and then we
shall select literature on Theosophy for further study
and enlightenment. The author hopes to stimulate a
taste for Theosophy. If he achieves this, his book
will have been worth writing.

Let, then, Theosophy be put to the test of its effect
on life, and especially on the everyday life common to
us all: a life made up of so-called trifles, yet always
so potent for joy or for sorrow, for happiness or for
misery, for hope or for despair.

The essence of everyday life is the fact that we are
born amidst surroundings which profoundly affect us;
and most of us take for granted that it is useless to
ask why we have been born, and why our surroundings
are what they happen to be. There we are, and there
the surroundings are, and the growing and changing
relations between the two are part of what we vaguely
call the evolutionary process; though we assume that
the nature of this process can be but a matter of faith
and hope so far as we ourselves are concerned.

Into all this ignorance and uncertainty Theosophy
steps with its three great principles:

1. Happiness in life depends on discovering the meaning
and purpose of life through a constant challenging of life's circumstances, and also through positive and constructive dissatisfaction
with ignorance.

2. Theosophy is the eternal answer to those questions about life which sooner or later must be asked and must be answered.

3. No answer is finally true until it has passed from the stage of belief to that of experience, from the stage of hypothesis to that of knowledge.

Theosophy also declares:

1. That everything we see around us, in whatever kingdom of Nature, is eternally growing.

2. That there is a ladder of growing, on one or another of the innumerable rungs of which everything is standing, and from which everything is slowly moving to the rung above.

3. That everything, everywhere, is sowing and reaping experience, and that as it grows it leaves nothing behind, but takes with it all its sowings and all its reapings.

4. That we who are in the human kingdom have in us, therefore, the fruits of all experience acquired in the kingdoms through which we have so far passed.

5. That the rungs still to be reached, like coming events, cast their shadows before, and exercise upon us a gravitational influence. Thus the future draws us forward as past and present push us on.

Let us now see what Theosophy says when brought into contact with the two facts of birth and of environment.

First, that birth itself is a new episode in a process of growth or unfoldment whereby the individual—and each living thing is essentially an individual—passes through the varying darknesses of ignorance, sorrow, unhappiness, despair, to an eventual eternal sunshine of Peace and Power.

That in being born we are being reborn, taking up again the thread of life in this outer world after a period of rest and re-creation in that condition of consciousness quite rightly called Heaven.

That when a particular life is over, and is closed by what we call death, there is not written " The End " or " Conclusion ", but " To be continued in his or her next ". Death is but a doorway leading to refreshment and to further unfoldment.

Second, that our surroundings, of whatever nature, are exactly what we need for our gradually unfolding growth. Mother, father, brothers, sisters, friends, faith, nationality, opportunities or the lack of them, the whole of the setting for birth and growth: all these are what we need in our present incarnation. In incarnations gone by there have been other settings, other opportunities, to meet the varying needs of varying stages of unfoldment, though probably within a more or less unchanging group of individuals marked by changing relationships. In incarnations to come settings and opportunities will change and change, the group still remaining more or less the same, but unfolding into truer comradeship. Until at last settings and opportunities have no more to teach, for we have mastered all their lessons.

That we must make the best of our surroundings, squeeze out of them, as they are, all possible opportunities, learn the lessons they are designed to teach.

That we must gradually absorb them, by utmost utilization, into better surroundings.

That no one in this outer world has perfect surroundings—surroundings which cannot be improved.

That the best way of exchanging existing surroundings for better ones, is to improve our relationship with each element in them, less by resignation to them, more by entering constructively into the spirit of them.

That there is not, as a rule, any occasion for running away from our surroundings, but rather for fulfilling them and using them to achieve their educative purposes.

We thus perceive that Theosophy tells us much which at present we do not know, may as yet be unable to believe, and have at present no means of knowing.

Few of us can say that we know this particular birth of ours to be only one of very many. Few of us can say that we recognize our surroundings as our teachers, guides, philosophers and friends.

Most of us are very likely to deny the possibility of knowledge of any particular birth before this one. We demand what we call " proof ", an almost physical vision of previous births, so that we can " see " them for ourselves, forgetting that even had we such vision it would not be long before we should declare that we had been hypnotized or in some other way deceived.

" Proof " needs two factors for its fulfilment—presentation and receptivity. However unchallengeable the presentation may be it must needs fade into the darkness of common disbelief if there be little or no receptivity to take its impress.

Receptivity depends upon experience, and before experience is finally achieved it passes through various stages. First, ignorance; second, the ringing of the changes upon ridicule, persecution, contempt, abhorrence—this is the stage of ignorance seeking its own survival; third, doubt; fourth, wonder; fifth, attraction; sixth, belief; seventh, experience itself, making real that which has so far been more or less unreal.

Proof impinges impotently upon ignorance; helplessly upon ridicule, persecution, contempt and abhorrence; ineffectively upon doubt; intriguingly upon wonder; sympathetically upon attraction; powerfully upon belief, and compellingly upon experience, since the very proof itself is part of the experience. But the wise man finds very little satisfaction in so-called "proof", for he knows that final proof takes its rise within him and never outside him, and that "proof" from outside can never be more than a sign-post pointing to a goal.

As for surroundings, it is the fashion to regard these as external to the individual, as comprising an environment in which he is fortuitously placed. He will affect his surroundings, and his surroundings will affect him. And the result of the interaction is just a matter for speculation, nothing more.

Science will explain that sometimes the individual overwhelms the environment, but that more often environment overwhelms the individual; that normally it is likely to be environment which exercises the predominating influence. But in either case it is a grand toss-up.

Theosophy reduces this chaos to cosmos by stating that in every detail an individual's surroundings not only are precisely as he has made them in previous births, and as he has been constructing them through all previous births, but are precisely what he needs for the next step in the process of his growth.

Whatever these surroundings may be—parentage, family, friends, faith, nationality, material circumstances, and so forth—they are of his own building, and are his own opportunity.

Theosophy denies the existence of misfits as between the individual and his surroundings. It states that since the object of evolution or growth is experience, to the end of happiness, power and peace, and since in fact there is no such thing as waste of what we call time—a word which really means occasion for opportunity—it follows that every circumstance of life is opportunity, is the knocking on the door of what we are by that which we need, are to become, next.

There is not a single circumstance of life with which an individual comes into contact, which is other than the larger seeking access to the less. The humblest object—chair, table, carpet, flower, animal, picture—calls, dumbly to most, to the few clamantly, for a finer relationship between itself and the individual. It calls for delicacy and understanding of handling and of use. It calls for purposiveness in its employment and, laugh though you may, for reverence.

Thus Theosophy gives value to everything, purpose to everything, and *life* to everything. In the dictionary of Theosophy certain words are non-existent—lifeless or inorganic, hopeless, helpless, useless; all other words expressive of futility or annihilation; all words expressive of a ceasing of purpose or of eternal damnation; and all words expressive of an unhappiness which is other than fleeting, or of any hatred or wrath which shall not sooner or later succumb to love.

Theosophy is indeed the Science of true values. It is the Science of true optimism. It is the Science of the wonderful worthwhileness of circumstances. It is the Science of the silver lining to all clouds, however black or sinister. It is the Science of all-pervading justice and love in Life. It is the Science of certainty. It is the Science of opportunity. It is the Science of success. It is the Science of Joy, of Peace, of ceaseless Delight.

Theosophy is more than any individual religion, for it is the Golden Chain which unites them all, and the Life which makes each of them real.

Theosophy is more than any individual science or philosophy, for it includes that which is necessarily beyond their frontiers. Sciences and philosophies must needs be, in no small measure, the reflections of their times. Theosophy as we have it is a reflection of the eternal.

Theosophy is more than the beliefs and opinions and convictions of any individual, for it expresses the individual in his completeness, as well as in his stages.

Theosophy is more than the past. It is more than the present. It adds to these the future.

Let us now watch Theosophy at work in the ordinary everyday details of the ordinary everyday lives of the vast majority of us—ordinary everyday people.

CHAPTER I

THE INDIVIDUAL YOU

You are born. Who is it that is born?

Without going into the necessarily complicated teachings of Theosophy regarding the origin of life and of individuality in it, it may be said that you are a pilgrim on your way from unawareness as to who you are to the discovery that in fact you are a King of Life, and to an eventual exercise of your Kingship.

For a partial and necessarily incomplete definition of a King of Life you have but to think of those to whom you look as great examples of human perfection. " How I wish I could be like . . ." and then the name of your most inspiring ideal. In ordinary everyday life you will sigh at the hopelessness of the wish. But Theosophy is the fairy godmother which replies, " So shall you be some day; and the more you determine the sooner the day."

Growth, of course, takes time, or why time? But you have already reached the level you now occupy, and it is to be hoped that you are aware of the fact that you have reached this level, even though you may rightly feel that you have not gone so very far, and that you are beginning to perceive before you heights you long to scale.

Theosophy tells you that the life now unfolded in you—a very definite individuality indeed—was in the far-off distant past entirely undeveloped. Through one state of consciousness after another—these states are ordinarily called kingdoms of Nature—the life which you now know as " I " slowly developed until it became possible for you to say " I ", and so to distinguish yourself definitely from your surroundings.

At first this " I " does not amount to very much. It has only just begun to be separate from all the other " I's " with which it has so far been associated for what may be called economy's sake. Theosophy says that hardly before reaching the human kingdom do these " I's " disentangle themselves from the particular mass of " I's " in the midst of which they have heretofore lived and moved and had their being. But the moment an individuality has reached the threshold of that state of consciousness which we call the human kingdom, it leaves the nest of the group and enters the business of life on its own.

To start with, therefore, the " I " is a comparatively poor affair, as witness the entirely undeveloped savage. But as birth succeeds birth the irresistible pressure of the unfolding quality in life, working from within the " I " no less than from without, causes slow but steady progress. It is here that Theosophy brushes aside the confusion between Freedom and Necessity.

These two words only have meaning as we think of the individual and the evolutionary process as distinct, so that there seems to be a kind of conflict between the individual and some external power. Theosophy identifies the individual with the external power which is the evolutionary process, so that so-called necessity becomes natural to the individual, part of his very nature, and freedom becomes power to achieve this natural, inborn necessity. In Theosophy, Necessity is represented by the word Kingship, and Freedom by the word Power. Far from there being any conflict between Freedom and Necessity, far from the individual being a mere pawn in a relentless game, Freedom is, in fact, the splendid servant of a marvellous Necessity; and the individual is thus a King in the becoming, using his Freedom to achieve the destiny which he himself has made his Necessity. In his aspect as an integral part of the One Life, he establishes a glorious, personal and universal necessity. As an individual, he endows himself with Freedom to realize the glory he has determined he shall not escape.

Here you now are, therefore, with your " I " at a certain stage of its development. If the future means little to you, if you are largely centred in the present or in the past, you may be immensely proud of your present " I " and of everyone of its constituent elements. You may be very proud of yourself, very contented with yourself. You may be proud of your aspirations, your ideals, your thoughts, your feelings, your activities. You may be in the grip of a static self-satisfaction. And its effect will be to cause you to regard yourself as immeasurably superior to all who have " I's " different from your own.

You will feel yourself to be " right ", and you will wonder how other people are unable to perceive that the only way to be right is to be like you. You will revel in your particular brand of religion, politics, habits, and all other characteristics of your individual stage of evolution. You will in fact be narrow, intolerant, and perhaps even piously, possibly compassionately, aggressive.

Theosophy seeks to endow you with a sense of proportion. It says to you: "So far so good; but be dynamic for the future that awaits you. Do not rest stagnant in the present." Theosophy calls upon you to have a joyous dissatisfaction with all that you are, without a single exception, however good some of that "all" may be; and urges you to be eager for the still finer "I" which you are to be—all the sooner if time be your servant, but all the later if time be your master. Why, says Theosophy, be content with a relatively small "I" when there are larger and larger unfoldments of that "I" waiting for your grasping?

The greatest obstacle Theosophy encounters in this connection is that embodied in the phrase: "I am quite content where I am." Let it be said without hesitation that Theosophy is also the Science of Discontent, but not of a grumbling, irritable, despairing, aggressive, thoroughly miserable, discontent. It is the Science of a delighted discontent, a discontent which is thrilled to think that there is something available to the present "I" far, far better than that which now characterizes it. An individual who is content where he is, is certainly not dead, but he is only half alive, for he is resisting contact with all that life has still to offer him. Instead of being part of the river, he insists on being a little stagnant pool in which pride seeks to usurp and kill the function of movement.

Theosophy helps you to enjoy the immense virility of this discontent, and to be ever eager to adventure into the future which in all certainty awaits you, describing that further to you in terms that glow and sparkle and allure.

Theosophy does more than this. It helps you to understand and to appreciate other people where they are, with their opinions, their forms of religion, their political views, their aspirations, their habits, their "I's". The world would be so much more happy, and so much more prosperous and peaceful, if we could learn to be as satisfied with other people as we are satisfied with ourselves.

Theosophy insists that it is not difference of religion, or of nationality, or of habits and customs, which marks differences in stage of evolution. Religions, races, nations, habits and customs, are but different classes in the great School of Life. Different stages of evolution are marked by differences in refinement, in nobility, in dignity, in generosity, in kindliness, in appreciation, in wisdom, in power, in the sense of the Brotherhood of all Life within the Fatherhood of Divine Purpose—defining the word "Divine" how you will.

But let us now go back to your birth, leaving for another chapter these questions of surroundings.

You are born in a baby body. What are you doing during babydom? Theosophy says that you are learning to become accustomed to your new physical body. And here let it be made clear that running as silver thread through all your relatively innumerable births is that which you call "I". The "I" is permanent though growing, but its vehicles change from birth to birth. Your "I" is very old indeed, almost indefinitely old. But you wear clean clothes as you embark birth after birth on life's adventure. As a baby you have a nice, clean, new body—small, of course, weak, more or less helpless—yet more or less potent with character according to your stage and type of evolution.

Now what is the purpose of this nice, clean, new body? To be the intermediary, or shall we say the channel, between your "I", and that outer life around you whence your "I" derives much of its nutriment.

When, at the end of your last birth, death came as a solicitous valet to help you to take off your old and worn-out garments, you retired for a space of time into a Heaven bath, which resembled in its power of refreshment the hot bath we know so well down here. In Heaven, says Theosophy a process of re-creation takes place. You readjust yourself to Life's eternal purposes from out of that semi-forgetfulness which must inevitably characterize your gradual conquest of life's more material regions as represented by this physical world of ours. You gain some glimpse, too, of the glory of the future which is yours. It is as if in the midst of darkness you were suddenly to perceive the rising sun and to witness all the splendid colours of its ascending blessing. Thus enthralled, and realizing that no part of life, even the most material, may be left uncon-quered if you would embody that future, you plunge desirously down into this world to resume a pilgrimage which in Heaven you know to be wondrous, though on earth it often seems very weary.

Into a physical body you come, because you must have a body of earth to contact earth's lessons. In the earlier years you gradually become accustomed to the new suit of clothes, though at first they do not seem to fit, especially when the teething process begins and you go through the aches and pains common to early childhood. Year by year with ever-increasing surety you learn to resume the old contacts through thought, feelings and emotions, and through the physical body itself.

Your old powers will renew their sway. Old tendencies will again dominate. Old associations will once more bind. Resuming the old movements, you will once more be in the full swing of the pendulum of your life, such swing, that is, as you are able, at your present stage of evolution, to give it.

You will gradually renew your old life, but differently; differently because the environment, the setting, is so very different from that in which your life was last lived many years, possibly many centuries, ago. How long ago? The period depends upon innumerable circumstances, one of which is how far advanced you happen to be on the pathway of life. Let us say, just for the sake of giving a number, from four to seven centuries ago. But the number may be far less or far more.

The fact of this difference of setting, of environment, is both the cause of, and the opportunity for, growth. Were you to perpetuate the same environment life after life, you would surely degenerate. It would be like marriage between persons too closely related. You are freshly equipped for the adventure of the new birth, and there is a new mode of environment in which the adventure takes place. So, under such favourable surroundings, on you go, taking up your life again, as regards the physical world, more or less where you left it off; though, indeed, the intervening period between the undressing we call death and the dressing we call birth carries us definitely onwards, so that we do not begin quite at the point where we left off.

Then comes the work of utilizing every constituent element in your surroundings for the further progress you are intended to make during this particular birth. Here Theosophy helps in a wonderful way, for it makes very clear both where you are and what you have to do. After a comparatively brief study of Theosophy, in the classic literature available, you will gain a fairly clear idea as to who you are, what kind of person you are, what has, so far, been your general pathway, and, of infinitely greater importance, whither you are directing your course.

Knowing these things more and more accurately, you become more and more able to take effective advantage of all the available force clothed in the myriad forms of circumstance which surround you. If you know whence you have come, what kind of individual you are, and more or less what kind of individual your " I " has designed himself to become, you will be far more constructively scientific in your relations with your surroundings. You will be an individual

THE INDIVIDUAL YOU

who knows what he is about, not just a straw at the mercy of the winds.

In other words, you begin with greater force, speed and precision to develop character, and character is the vital essence of happiness and power.

So here you are, an old " I " in a fresh suit of clothes, down here again because you wanted to come, knowing that down here is part of the field on which Life's victory is to be won. Theosophy comes powerfully to your aid as you desire with increasing insistence to "know what it is all about". Theosophy tells you why you are a baby, why the baby grows as he does, what he is, in fact, doing in the course of his strange, unintelligible little life, what he is gradually coming to and how the best use can be made of the baby situation.

In the next Chapter, Theosophy will have most interesting things to say about parents and family, for these too come with you out of the past. From one point of view, a new birth brings new surroundings. But from another point of view it brings only old surroundings newly dressed. Let us now see how this works out in regard to parents and family.

CHAPTER II

YOUR PARENTS AND FAMILY

HAVING been duly born, the question is not so much —to whom you have been born; but, rather—why you have been born to *them*.

Is it haphazard, as if the individual to be born, or rather to be re-born, blindly draws a couple of parents out of a lucky (sometimes an unlucky) dip? Theosophy denies that there is anything haphazard about the choice of parents, and therefore about the choice of children. On the contrary, the fact is that each individual moves within a comparatively limited circle of other individuals throughout the whole of his evolutionary process. The same people have over and over and over again to do the duty of—or, to be more accurate, to ring the changes on—father, mother, brother, sister, uncle, aunt, cousin, grandfather, grandmother, son, daughter, nephew, niece, and any other relationships you may be able to conceive, including that of friendship.

It follows, therefore, that your father in this life has probably been a relative many times before, and certainly a comparatively close friend; the same applies to your mother, and to all other members of your present family, as well as to those outside the family circle.

Thus we pick up the threads, in the new birth, not only of activities, thoughts, feelings, emotions, but also of relationships. It is by no means an exaggeration to say that your relatives in this life have, during the long past, filled every possible kind of relationship towards you, even though each one may seem so particularly suited (or unsuited!) to the role he or she plays today.

You may not be able to imagine that a somewhat prim and old-fashioned maiden aunt was once one of your most wayward children, or perhaps even a wayward brother. But such may well have been the case. The temperament an individual displays during one particular life is by no means necessarily his or her fundamental and invariable temperament. In fact, the reverse is far more necessary and true. The purpose of evolution is to develop, on the whole, an all-round perfection, no lopsided extravagance. Sooner or later, the most hardened quality or weakness must give way to its opposite, both for the sake of complete experience and of that perfect flexibility which, residing on the heights, knows how to descend into the valleys without losing even the faintest fragrance of the mountains.

Finally, the destination of each one of us is an Everest, but there can be no perfect appreciation of Everest unless we have also descended to the depths of its antithesis. Incidentally, this fact helps us to have the broadest sympathy and understanding for all weakness and ignorance, since even these are stages on the way to glorious heights. Incidentally, too, another word becomes eliminated from the Theosoph-ical dictionary—wickedness. Difficult as it may be to believe, there is, when one comes to analyse motives and actions, no such state of consciousness as that expressed in the term " wickedness ". Ignorance, yes; weakness, yes; but nothing more.

All this is a digression. It is merely to mark the fact, so easy to miss, that relationships and the various characteristics they display are like the picture we see for a moment in a kaleidoscope. A shake of the kaleidoscope, and the same pieces form a picture totally different. Save, perhaps, in the much earlier stages of the evolutionary process, where the changes are very slow and gradual, each new birth produces a new picture, though ever expressing an eternal theme; and an individual in one picture may, in the new one, appear almost unrecognizable.

Yet, running through each bead of birth is a unique golden thread of individuality. From the beginning of time this golden thread existed, coiled, as one might say, within itself unmanifest, unindividualized, unborn. Then comes the impetus into growth—we need not here concern ourselves with the origin of such impetus. The golden thread uncoils and threads on to itself bead after bead of descent into birth so that a necklace of Divine Perfection may at last be fashioned. How much of his or her own individual necklace has each one of us threaded with the beads of experience? In the earlier stages, the beads must needs, temporarily, be rough and ill-fashioned. But at last each bead attains perfection, and the Circle of Eternal Life becomes complete.

To resume. Here is the baby boy or girl, but not a baby " I ", be it remembered, in the midst of a number of members of a family whom he has known over and over again in the past, but whom he does not, in all probability, remember in the present. He will not, save exceptionally, be able to say, as speech comes to him: " But you were not my father last time! You were my very tiresome daughter, who gave me far more trouble than I am ever likely to give you!" Nor will he in all likelihood be able to say: " How strange that you should be my mother this time! You and I were lovers last life, were married, had a large family, and lived to a ripe old age!" He will probably not be able to remember these erstwhile relationships. And this forgetfulness is indeed divine in its mercy.

If at our comparatively imperfect stage of growth we remembered these relationships, we should also remember all the circumstances which they involved. And we should be in danger of perpetuating the old relationships, many of which we should be well advised radically to change in quality. We should remember the old mistakes we had made, the old injuries we had inflicted, the old wrongs we had suffered, the old debts we may still have yet to receive.

Memory is a powerful weapon. In the hands of the wise it will beautify. In the hands of the ignorant it will injure both its wielder and those whom it re-members. In the hands of the wise, memory will be tender and forgiving even where there be injury and wrong for which Law must needs exact redress. In the hands of the ignorant memory will be harsh and revengeful, and will demand, to the last fragment, its pound of flesh.

It is mercifully ordained that our memories re-main poor, even though their reflections may be perceived in instinctive likes and dislikes. Only when we grow spiritually old enough can we be safely trusted with an all-penetrating and unbroken memory.

So the past is comparatively a blank, and ordinarily we do not and cannot think of our relatives in this life in any other roles than those they now are occupying. Yet the past will not be entirely denied. There is the favourite child. There is the specially loved parent. There is the friend beyond all other friends. There is the grandmother of whom we may be afraid, and the grandfather who is our most intimate confidant. Always are there sympathies and antipathies for which we are entirely unable to account, for which there is no reason because there is no memory. Memory is so much an essential ingredient of accurate reasoning faculty.

Be all this as it may, your entry into your family is the resumption of old ties. You have known everybody in the family before, and well. With everybody you have been intimately associated for a very long time. With everybody you will continue your journey onwards into the future, until you form a small circle of perfect brotherhood, part of that universal circle which includes your circle and innumerable others. It may be easier to understand the idea of this universal circle if you remember that each member of your own circle is a part of a circle with which you are only indirectly connected. And if you extend this idea far enough you will see that universality is the natural and inevitable consequence of the particularity to which you yourself belong.

It should, however, be stated that by no means the whole of your own particular comradeship must of necessity have birth when you have yours. There may be many relatives and friends out of incarnation, who are not taking birth on this occasion, or who will be incarnating later, so that you will not meet them down here until this birth of yours is already well on its way. You may not meet them at all this life, though during what we call sleep you will have many happy gatherings of the members of your particular evolutionary family party.

It may well be that your nearest and dearest are, for the best of reasons, away from you, so far as regards the physical plane. You may or may not feel a sense of incompleteness. This will depend upon the strength of your memory. Do not imagine that you are always complete as to numbers in each incarnation which you yourself happen to take. But somewhere, says Theosophy, there is not only a solidarity, but, even more, a unity of your individual comradeship which neither birth nor death, nor presence nor absence, can affect. Somewhere, your family of relatives and friends is ever complete. Somewhere, the golden threads of your individualities form an indissoluble and perfect cord of comradeship, even though at any particular time a particular thread may be busy with a bead of birth, while some other threads may not.

Somewhere? Where? The answer to that question, so reasonable and so insistent, will be found in the literature of Theosophy, which probes the depths and not just those surfaces with which alone this book must needs be concerned. There is a world where brotherhood ever reigns, where friendship is never broken, where separation has no being, where sadness has no place. That world is the real world, and in it your company of comrades is ever together. But it is still a limited world when it should be a world which knows no barriers. And to the end of making limitless so glorious a world, you and all the rest of life in manifestation take birth after birth, struggle time after time with ignorance, sorrow, hardship, separation, frustration, in order that their darkness may disappear, their barriers be removed, and the way become clear for the perpetual shining, in all worlds, of the Light of that inner world which for so long is dim and feeble in the outer. Theosophy is the reflection down here of the life of that real world. Not yet knowing, only groping, we may think Theosophy to be but teaching, hypothesis, theory, philosophy, speculation. But some there are who know Theosophy to be fact, to be the expression, in necessarily imperfect form, of the One and Universal Life, for Theosophy's Truths have become their experience.

Let Theosophy be as an electric torch, throwing light upon those facts which, as you understand them more and more, will enable you to use every circumstance, be it pleasant or disagreeable, to a happy and fruitful consummation, as much for your comrades as for yourself.

We will now consider the various incidents of your life as expressed in terms of education, ease and disease of circumstances, opportunities, disabilities, tendencies, and *hoc genus omne*.

CHAPTER III

YOUR EDUCATION

WHAT and whom does an educational system educate? Ordinarily, no one cares *whom*, for the very
simple reason that most people cannot even begin to
answer the question. Even in these so-called civilized
days every child is educated as if he were no body in
particular and everybody in general. It makes for
simplicity and convenience of method and organiza-
tion, no doubt, but for infinite hardship to the child
and for very poor service to the nation concerned.

Theosophy has, as must by this time be apparent,
much to answer to the question: " Whom does the
educational system educate? "

First of all no " whom " is just a bolt from the
blue. He is an independent, and indeed a unique,
individuality which has already travelled a long way
on the path of life, has reached a certain level in the
human kingdom after having gathered the experiences
appropriate to the animal, vegetable and mineral
kingdoms, is climbing still higher in the human kingdom, and will some day emerge, as will all other
human beings, a King of Men.

Second, each " whom " has behind him his own
distinct and different mode of evolution, however

much he may seem to be like all other "whoms".
Each "whom" has his own specific temperament, his
own specific genius, his own specific place in the great
Purpose and Plan.

Therefore, when we are educating a child, we are
educating an age-old soul, and we are educating a
unique individuality. The physical body may be
young, but that is all the youth there is about the
child, whom we so call after his body because we
know nothing about his soul, and may even, in our
ignorance, deny that he possesses one.

The wise parent, therefore, and the wise teacher,
will remember the existence of the soul, will remember
that they are educating a very old and experienced
traveller who really knows what he wants, and who
expects parent and teacher to discover his needs. By
their wisdom or by their clumsiness they may make or
mar, for this old traveller, his present adventure in
our midst.

The business of parent and teacher is to help the
individuality as rapidly as possible to make effective
contact with his new vehicles. Parent and teacher
have been longer in their physical bodies than he has.
They have more physical plane experience, and should
place this experience at his disposal, partly to guard
him against unnecessarily falling into dangers and
difficulties, and partly to help him, as far as they can,
to short cuts to the necessary physical plane experience. But they must never coerce him, save in the
more serious emergencies, still less may they try to
make him a replica of themselves as to thoughts,
opinions and feelings. They must help him to

re-discover in this outer world his own eternal life and to continue its unfoldment—however different it may be from their own modes of living and of unfoldment. They must help him to become, not a copy of themselves, but a continuation of himself.

It is certainly true that most members of the human family still have some distance to travel before they reach the point of being able to express in their very physical bodies accurate and undimmed reflections of their coming Kingship. But the reflections are there, and the wiser the education the more quickly will come the dawning of the kingly splendour.

Parent and teacher should at least try to help the child to discover this Kingship, less by endeavouring to guess what kind of Kingship may be latent, more by themselves becoming increasingly alive with something of Kingship's royalty, so that the royalty in them may call in its common language to the royalty in the child.

So often has the age-old traveller been compelled, Theosophy teaches us, to abandon effective use of his new body simply because careless and clumsy educational workmen have failed to help fashion it in terms of dignity, refinement and happiness. So often the age-old traveller finds his channels stopped up with rubbish when they should be free for his power. Still more often he finds his vehicle becoming dull through ill-usage, through fear, perhaps even through cruelty. True, there is no absolute, though certainly there is relative, injustice in all this to the child. These unhappinesses must somehow be due to him. But

neither parent nor teacher should lend himself to be
the channel for their descent. Let them come if they
must, but we need be no party to their coming, unless
it be the unescapable law.

It is a tremendous responsibility to be a parent or a
teacher. It is a tremendous responsibility to conceive a
body for the dwelling of an old friend—as every child
indeed is. Parent and teacher have in some measure
the power to make a birth either a blessing or a curse,
to help the individual to make rapid strides, or to
hold him back.

Theosophy has very much to say about this
" whom " for which there is no room in the pages
of this book. Theosophical education is indeed a
science in itself.

As to *what* an educational system educates, here
again the general conception is that we are educating
a mixture composed of physical body, feelings and
emotions, and mind, with possibly just a trace of
something more.

Once more, Theosophy reduces this comparative
chaos to a very ordered cosmos. We are told that
the individuality uses a number of distinct bodies,
one of which is the physical body through which
ordinarily there is communication with the outer
world by means of the various senses. But there are
other bodies, no less definite than the physical body.
There is the emotional body in which the feelings and
the emotions live and move and have their being.
There is the mind body, in which the mental functions
exist. There is the intuitional body, specialized for the
habitation and expression of that state of consciousness

which we call the intuition. And there are higher bodies still.

All these interpenetrate the physical body though they are larger in size and decreasingly dense in texture. Each has its own separate existence, although there is a very large measure of inter-dependence. When the physical body disintegrates at death the other bodies survive, and may even be carried forward into the new birth, though this is rare. Generally, these other bodies disintegrate in their turn, and the individuality wears clean and fresh mental clothes, clean and fresh emotional clothes, as he wears clean and fresh physical clothes.

But all clothes are shaped to his eternal individuality-pattern. Each " I " has his own style and his own experience, which his clothes more or less embody.

So, when we ask what we are educating, we see that we are educating various kinds of consciousness; at once independent and most closely related and interdependent.

The question then arises as to whether we start educating them all at once, or whether there is some kind of order for their development.

Obviously, the physical body must have first attention. It develops first and upon its right education depends to no small degree the right functioning of all the other bodies; for it is their channel of communication with that outer world through which they too have to grow.

From the beginning to the end of the educational system the education of the physical body must receive constant, and indeed, with the education of the emotional body, dominant attention.

The body of the feelings and emotions is, with the physical body, the heart of the whole family of bodies. Without exception, we all live the most important part of our lives in our physical bodies and in our emotions. Physical we obviously are. Emotional we are no less, though many people, who pride themselves on their cold-bloodedness or on their dominantly mental outlook, will furiously deny this truth. However much attention we may rightly pay to the physical body, we must pay no less attention to the emotional body so that it may become controlled and purposeful. An individual who has his emotions under due control, not starved into rigidity but flexible to noble purposes, and whose physical body is a fine servant rather than a wayward master, is indeed well equipped to make his life a stepping stone to a greater height of achievement.

When the word " attention " is used, it is meant to convey an education in grace, in refinement, in subordination to the will (which is the individual), in dignity. The physical body must be rhythmic, supple, capable of enduring fatigue and deprivation—a horse requiring constant care but giving instant obedience. Of course, there may be some whose physical bodies start with handicaps. All that can be done is to minimize these to the utmost, and to educate the other bodies in cheerfulness and courage.

The emotional body must be educated to give accommodation to fine feelings and fine emotions alone. To an emotional body rightly educated, selfishness, anger, vulgarity, crudeness, passion of the coarser grade, all ignoble desires, must be unpleasant. There should be very few emotional bodies still needing the experience of hatred for their unfolding. Delight in, and as far as possible the creation of, the beautiful, whether of beautiful forms or of beautiful attitudes, should be the objective of emotional education. How little of such education is there in schools and colleges today!

It is, perhaps, necessary to say that education means, Theosophically speaking, what it says—the drawing out from within, with the help of the without, that which is awaiting unfoldment in these various reflection-bodies of the eternal soul. Environment knocks at the door. Power waits for release. Education is the link between the two, and its work is to help in the formation of, or rather in the strengthening of, character, attitude, ability to discriminate with increasing accuracy between the less useful and the more, the less true and the more, the less beautiful and the more. Every so-called fact, appertaining to no matter what subject, is really to this end; though it will surely be admitted that the "facts" with which we so often forcibly feed our educational victims have very little title to the name. When we speak of giving information, all we can actually mean is that we are giving the latest theories about certain aspects of life. How much more effective education would be if it were to lay less stress on forms and facts, and infinitely more on life and attitude.

If Theosophy be asked what about Freedom, the reply is instant. Freedom certainly. No attempt on

the part of parent or teacher to coerce the tender
shoots of the new bodies, to force them, to train
them in the likeness of the elder. No cruelty. No
education through fear—the two words are mutually
contradictory. No punishment, though sometimes
restraint. Freedom, yes; but ordered, purposeful
freedom. Freedom to grow in the light of the
Kingship-to-be. Freedom to become the Fire pre-
saged in the spark which, myriads of aeons ago, set
aglow the fuel of form in manifestation. Freedom
to move straightly forward. Freedom to spend time,
but not to waste it.

In a sentence, the freedom the bodies need is
freedom to co-operate perfectly with the individual—
the " I "—who is their king, freedom to do his will,
and to help to fulfil his purposes. How difficult for
parent or teacher to know the will of the lord when
they can hardly even understand the nature of his
servants. But such is the duty of both, and they
must, through affection and patience and intuition,
do the best they can.

We then come to the mind body, a body of
importance, but of no greater importance than its
emotional and physical comrades.

Perhaps accuracy and keenness of judgment are
the most important qualities to be educated. Knowledge the mind body must have, of course. But
knowledge changes so rapidly in these days that one
hesitates to say that the mind body must have facts.
Are there any facts at all? Perhaps it would be
more accurate to say that the mind body must as
fully as possible be in touch with tendencies in every

department of life, learning to hold them lightly so that out of them may emerge as time passes truer tendencies, until at last the fundamentally right direction shall have been taken and the Path of Wisdom reached.

Science itself is beginning to realize that the abstract more truly mirrors the Real than the concrete, and is tending in the direction of the abstract in its search for Truth.

The body of the mind must be educated to distinguish easily between that which, for it, is true and that which, for it, is false—truth and falsehood being largely relative to the individual. It must be educated to discern the Real amidst the unreal, Light amidst the darkness. Thus is it being helped to exercise its supreme function of accumulating material, of choosing the useful, and discarding the useless.

There are higher states of consciousness which also need educating. The intuitional consciousness is mainly dependent on experience for its nutriment and functioning. There is also the state of consciousness in which vision dwells. Vision, the power to see in the distance the splendour of life awaiting recognition and conquest, is of priceless value, and should in every possible way be encouraged by familiarizing the individual with the lives of those who, manifestly, have possessed the power of vision in substantial measure.

In whatever body the process of education is taking place, it must never be forgotten that we are not writing on a clean sheet, but upon a sheet already well marked by the countless experiences through which the individual has passed before he reached his present stage of growth. He is already full of tendencies, equipped to a certain extent with knowledge, faculties, aspirations, and, of course, weaknesses and inhibitions. It is the business of the parent and the teacher to seek to intuit these, so that the educative process may, as far as possible, take into account what has gone before and is already there.

A special warning may be given against trying to coerce or persuade the young bodies to swallow whole that which each should masticate before swallowing. Many parents and teachers have their own well-defined beliefs and convictions. They may have their own cut-and-dried rigidities as regards religion. They may be sure they are right, and that unless these young bodies accept these rigidities they will be lost.

Nobody is more than a little right. Everybody is far more ignorant, let us even say wrong, than he thinks he is. There are many, many more roads of righteousness than the one any particular individual is travelling.

It is thus of the highest importance, while setting before the child some definite conception of life, on no account to insist that it shall be swallowed whole. The truth is that nothing is ever swallowed whole. The parent or teacher may think it is, because the child seems to conform, perhaps does conform. But such conformity is only for the time being. The child has not in fact swallowed the conception. He cannot. It is in his cheek, and when the appropriate moment comes, out will come the conception, all the more rejected because it has been held ignorantly and possibly unwillingly. We have every right and every duty to give a child the benefit of our experience. But we must learn to realize that only his own experiences can be of any real value to him. And we must help him to these and not to our own.

In these days education is more directed towards analysis, dissection and criticism, using this word in its generally accepted meaning, than towards appreciation. Education for appreciation should be our motto in this department, so that, while first we learn to appreciate the nearer and the more familiar, which is often for the very reason of its nearness all the more difficult to appreciate—familiarity breeds contempt— we may also try to learn to appreciate that which is farther away and, possibly, strange. Human beings are very much like animals in being extraordinarily tenacious of the herd spirit. No doubt this spirit has its value and its purpose, but it has, too, distinct limitations. Education largely falls short of its duty if, while utilizing the herd spirit to its true purpose, it does not provide a means for due transcendence of that which, after all, is intended to be an experience we must take with us on our way, and not a place in which we must entrench ourselves against all advance.

It is easy enough to find fault, especially if we are narrow in our outlook upon life. Many people are in a constant state of antagonism towards all that is outside their own immediate conception of life. They find fault with other people's religions, with other people's nationalities, with other people's opinions

and habits and customs, seemingly unable to realize
that other people find fault no less extensively with
theirs.

We have to learn to find good and not fault.
There is as much good, on the whole, in other people
as there is in ourselves. Their religions are as good.
Their nationalities are as good. Their habits and
customs are as good. Their opinions are as good.

Let education be for understanding and not for
misunderstanding, as it so largely is to-day.

As for the details of education, only a bare outline
can be given here.

Certain occupations are vital. Certain qualities are
essential. We must educate for courage, for truth,
for enthusiasm, for chivalry. Let the means be what
you will, there is no real education which does not
evoke in every child a measure of all four.

To the end of developing such powers, we must
educate in craftsmanship, music, games, physical
development, singing, handicrafts, cooking, first aid,
general housecraft, the science of sex, good citizenship
—national and super-national; and we must remember
that to educate for leisure is at least seventy-five
per cent of our duty.

As for a career, in these modern days of competition, depression and confusion, it is almost impossible
to avoid hardship. Theosophy in its psychological
aspect recognizes seven distinct types of evolution,
one of which is dominant in each individual, the
others being sub-dominant. To develop the type is
to follow the line of least resistance and therefore of
quickest unfoldment. But types are hidden from our

discovering, and individuals of one type find themselves engaged in activity belonging to a type entirely different.

The priest finds himself a merchant. The merchant finds himself a lawyer. The soldier finds himself a clerk. The statesman finds himself a mechanic. The teacher finds himself a merchant. The servant finds himself a ruler. And some find themselves unemployed!

Surely it is obvious that a nation cannot be run efficiently unless its governing personnel is composed of men and women who are temperamentally fitted for their duties. Surely it is obvious that an individual cannot live efficiently unless he is unfolding his own individual and eternal line of development.

Yet we still see little if any further than the surface, and a happy-go-lucky education is followed by a happy-go-lucky life. What wonder the recessions! What wonder war!

All the greater need for Theosophy to help us to discover who and what we are.

It is not inappropriate, in a chapter on education, to call attention to a truth on which Theosophy alone lays stress—the truth that those who to-day are elders will at no distant time become the young to those who will then be old. The older generation has but a temporary advantage over youth as regards years and experience. The young will themselves in due course gain both years and experience, and the old will go onwards into a new youth, expecting their then elders, who are to-day's youth, to help them along as it is to be hoped the older generation is at present helping youth along. Let youth be reverent to age, and age no less reverent to youth. Each needs the other. Together they can, being complementary one to the other, fulfilling one another, make life easier and more fruitful for each.

Youth needs age. Age needs youth. Youth will become age. Age will become youth. If only this truth could be realized, and could be made a potent factor in the lives of young and old, the lives of the young would become infinitely more effective, and the lives of the old infinitely more useful and more joyous. There is nothing in age to be shunned. There is nothing in youth to be despised. There is everything in each for which the other may indeed be thankful. There should be, and there need be, no water-tight compartments excluding the one from the other. Theosophy, while appreciating youth and age at their respective values, regards both as but aspects of growth, as but different phases of one movement. Specifically, teacher has as much to learn from student, as student from teacher. Teacher and taught are in fact learning and growing, together. Who, in terms of life, shall venture to say who is teacher and who is student! And when the teacher understands that he, too, is no less a child than the children he teaches, then indeed, and then alone, will he have begun to enter into the spirit of the science of education.

A final word. The entire objective of education may be summed up in the one word " Reverence ". Reverence is the way and the end of growth, the power and purpose of evolution, the joy and the peace of life. To know is to be reverent, and the wider the knowledge the more universal a reverence which excludes not even the lowliest manifestations of life. We must have reverence between man and woman, elder and younger, saint and sinner, strong and weak, human and sub-human kingdoms of nature, reverence for all life in all its innumerable modes of manifestation, be these beautiful or ugly, savage or civilized.

Few of us are consistently reverent. But only as education stimulates reverence is it real and purposeful.

CHAPTER IV

YOUR LARGER FAMILY

You are probably well acquainted with your parents and other relatives. You are probably well acquainted with your friends and acquaintances. You feel a link with your co-religionists, and with those who are members of the nation to which you belong. Furthermore, you have perhaps some idea of con-sanguinity with other members of your race, with the group of nations of which your nation may form part.

As for humanity in the large, it probably means little or nothing to you save as a principle, an abstraction.

Now Theosophy declares that all life is One, no matter what may be its form. The life that flows in the veins of the Saviour flows in the veins of the most ignorant of individuals, and flows too in the veins of every denizen of every kingdom of nature. In one kingdom of nature life may still be in the seed. In the next higher kingdom it may have emerged into a shoot. In the next it may have advanced to the stage of the bud. And in a still higher kingdom the bud may be just beginning to unfold. Yet higher, and the opening bud may be taking on the semblance of a flower. And so onwards and upwards. There is but the one life, says Theosophy, in whatever stage of unfoldment it may be.

Hence there is the closest affinity in fact, though not necessarily in form, and still less in appearance, between all modes of manifestation, in every kingdom. This becomes all the more evident when we hear Theosophy declaring that the life in the highest of individuals has passed through the lowliest of forms and stages of manifestation on its upward way.

The higher the development the wider and fuller the experience. Not a single experience through which life in the mineral, vegetable, animal or human kingdom is passing, is unknown in one aspect or in another to an individual who has reached his Kingship. Not a single weakness, vice, hardship or sorrow, which life experiences, is, in one way or in another, unknown to such a King. His Kingship is fashioned out of the clay of a myriad of experiences, of a myriad of successes and failures, of a myriad of joys and sorrows. He has triumphed; therefore so shall we triumph wherever we are, and whoever we are.

In very truth, the great of whom we have heard, whom perchance we may have been fortunate enough to see, are to us, even though our ignorance may blind us to the knowledge of it, witnesses to the future that awaits us all. "Ye are Gods", says every Saviour; and so we are in our life's nature, and therefore in the becoming. This truth should, as it becomes increasingly understood, help us to grow in increasingly right relationship to our surroundings, to appreciate them better, to live with them in a more brotherly spirit, and above all to cease to inflict upon them suffering for the sake of any fancied advantage to ourselves.

There is the closest of blood relationship between ourselves in the human kingdom and the forms of life we see around us in the animal, vegetable and mineral kingdoms. We are blood brothers to every animal, to every flower, tree and weed, to every rock and stone, to mountain and to mud. At first, this idea may seem nothing less than objectionable. We shall feel inclined to say that we do not in the least degree feel brotherly towards this, that, or the other form. We do not even feel brotherly to a large number of forms in our own, human, kingdom. It is possible to feel brotherly to a few who are near and dear to us. But it is not possible to feel brotherly to all and sundry.

The objection is natural at the stage of evolution which most of us have reached. But because we cannot yet feel the brotherhood it does not follow that therefore the brotherhood is non-existent. On the contrary, the more highly evolved the individual the more sure is he of the universal brotherhood of all life.

Birth into this outer world is sometimes called a process of adjustment. Adjustment to what? To the real, to the true, to the eternal, to the peace which passeth understanding, to joy that knows no change. Adjustment to true relationship between life and life, form and form, kingdom of nature and kingdom of nature. Adjustment to a life of peace, of understanding, of comradeship, of service, without distinction of stage of evolution. The larger family of each one of us is the whole world, every human being in it, every creature in it. And sooner or later we must learn to live in friendship with the whole of creation, treating each life in it reverently.

We must learn to treat with reverence and with refinement every form, less for the sake of the form, more for the sake of the indwelling and uprising life. There is no reason why we should not use, where necessary or expedient both for the used as well as for the user, but we must never abuse. To abuse is the great danger when might assumes licence over helplessness. Reverence, as was pointed out in the chapter on education, is the supreme virtue, the supreme power, for it contains within itself the flower of right relationship and of perfect adjustment.

We should be able to draw very near to those who are, with us, members of the human kingdom. To all intents and purposes we are at the same stage of evolution. We are treading the way together. We have to live in close association. We very much depend upon one another. Members of the human kingdom ought to be, and some day must be, very good friends and understanding comrades, not in spite of, but because of, such differences as separate them. We can well afford to be tolerant of each other's weaknesses and shortcomings, because for each shortcoming and weakness of another we are almost certain to have something to correspond in our own individual natures. It is easy to find fault with others. It ought to be still easier to find fault with ourselves, for we know ourselves better than we can possibly know others. But we need not really find fault with anyone, not even with ourselves, save sometimes and rarely in order to note a defect which needs adjusting.

We should also be able to draw near to members of the animal kingdom who are not, after all, so very far away from ourselves. These are our younger brethren, and have therefore the right to our protection and guidance. It may well be said that we have every right to restrain them from unduly interfering with us, to keep them in their due place. But this should not prevent us from bestowing upon them our reverence in the shape of gentleness and helpfulness. Most members of the animal kigdom are working their way towards the human kingdom. We have gone before them, and they are following after us. Let us give them our aid, as those who have gone before us so generously accord their aid to us.

Cruelty is inconceivable to the evolved individual. The infliction of pain upon younger brethren for the satisfaction of an elder is inconceivable to the evolved individual. To take away from a younger brother that which he has in order that an older brother may enjoy his own life more abundantly is inconceivable to the evolved individual. This does not mean that occasion may not arise to kill in self-defence. But it does mean that the human kingdom has no right selfishly to fatten on the kingdom of its brothers the animals.

The same principle applies to the relations of the human with the vegetable kingdom. Theosophy lays no greater stress than on the principle of the avoidance of ugliness. To prostitute an animal to human convenience, save in definite and grave emergency, is ugly and sordid; and there are many human beings who would not admit that any emergency, however urgent, could possibly justify such ugliness.

To avoid ugliness towards the vegetable kingdom is to avoid wanton destruction; is to avoid associating ugliness with it—as we so often do in our advertising mania; is to avoid treating with indifference such members of the kingdom as we uproot or pluck to provide satisfaction for our decorative and so-called artistic instincts; is to avoid the superstition that life in this vegetable kingdom is practically of no account and may be dealt with anyhow.

The life we now cherish in ourselves has had to pass through both vegetable and animal kingdoms. Let us give the lower the best chance we can, and the best chance is respect, kindliness, service.

No less must ugliness be avoided as regards the mineral kingdom. Our life has passed through this kingdom too. We owe it a debt, we owe it a service, as we owe debt and service to the vegetable and animal kingdoms; and the life in it is working its way onwards to pass through the kingdoms beyond.

To avoid ugliness towards the mineral kingdom is to avoid ugly material forms, forcing the life in this kingdom to look through ugliness upon the outer world. To fashion ugliness in stone, in clay, in steel or iron, or in any other substance belonging to the mineral kingdom, is to prostitute that kingdom to ugliness and to make it harder for the life in it to unfold. It is, of course, true that most of us have very little power to distinguish between ugliness and grace, and the commercial spirit has in no small measure had the effect of placing a premium upon the ugly. Yet the graceful and the beautiful can be as cheap as the ugly, cheaper in the long run because their appeal is so much greater.

If we could get rid of ugliness from commerce, from the kitchen and from the household generally, from our towns and cities, and above all from so-called art, we should be well on the way to a happier world. For the happiness of the human kingdom is not the sole essential for the world's happiness. The mineral kingdom must be happy in its own degree. The vegetable kingdom must be happy in its own degree. The animal kingdom must be happy in its own degree. There is but one brotherhood of all life, says Theosophy, and no part can be happy at the expense of any other part. Either we grow together, or we do not grow. There is no true happiness which is not a happiness shared, which is not a happiness in which there exists no ingredient inimical to happiness in any other part of the brotherhood.

It is impossible to purchase our own happiness with the coin of a pain inflicted on life around us. There may seem to be a fleeting gain, but the gain is illusory, and nemesis must sooner or later overtake the individual who imagines he can trample upon other life in order to establish his own. It is impossible to add to your own life by subtracting life from others. For a short period this may seem to be achieved. But sooner or later you will be compelled not only to subtract whatever you have added, with painful interest for the forced loan, but also to make that sacrifice for others which you have been at pains to demand from them. Such is the Law of Adjustment, whereby the ignorance of man is balanced by the justice of life.

Throughout this chapter we have so far been considering the mineral, vegetable, animal and human kingdoms. Vis-a-vis to the human kingdom we have been considering the sub-human kingdoms. But should we not be able to envisage super-human kingdoms as much beyond the evolutionary stage of the human kingdom, as the human kingdom itself is in advance of the sub-human kingdoms?

Does life stop short at the summit of the human kingdom where we perceive the greater men and women of our human world? Is there nothing greater that life can achieve than our humanity? Are there no heights greater than those of the human kingdom? We know that there are heights greater than those to be found in the mineral kingdom, than the diamond, the emerald, the ruby, the sapphire; heights greater than those to be found in the vegetable kingdom, than the noblest tree, the most gorgeous flower; heights greater than those to be found in the animal kingdom, than the most highly intelligent animal, the most faithful creature near and dear to the heart of man.

Should we not also know that there are heights greater than those to be found in the human kingdom, than the most splendid saint, the most chivalrous hero, the most far-sighted genius?

Fortunately, Theosophy gives us circumstantial information regarding certain of the heights beyond mankind.

First, we are told that there are well-defined kingdoms beyond the human kingdom, differentiated one from another by varying degrees of expansion of consciousness or life, as are our four kingdoms one from another.

Second, we are told that we too, as we grow, shall enter these kingdoms one after another, as we have entered kingdom after kingdom below.

Third, we are told that the citizens of these kingdoms are intent upon helping to the uttermost of their power those who are growing in kingdoms they themselves have already transcended. And we are further told that not only can we know them, as we grow fit to know them, but that they are willing from time to time to take as special students some of the more promising of their younger brethren in the human kingdom. This they do in order to gain more quickly recruits for the kingdom beyond the human, not for the personal advantage of the individual selected, but that one more individual may the sooner become free to serve the world with wisdom and with power.

In each kingdom of nature an individual life begins at the bottom and rises gradually to the top. In Theosophical literature details are given as to the way in which the life which has reached kingship in any particular kingdom dies from that kingdom to be born into the kingdom above. Then comes the learning of the lessons of the new kingdom, slowly

and often painfully acquired. Then again death from
that kingdom, or let us rather say ascension into the
kingdom of nature beyond. Such death, or ascension,
awaits us when we have learned to be kings in the
human kingdom; and there are those to help us,
when we are approaching kingship, to tread still more
quickly our way, so that ere long we may become
citizens of a superhuman kingdom beyond.

Incarnation after incarnation we die in order to live
more abundantly. From kingdom to kingdom we
die in order to enter and achieve the larger life of the
kingdom beyond.

Wherever we see genius, heroism, saintliness, or
any other noble quality, allied to a knowledge of the
eternal wisdom of life, and dedicated to the service of
all, irrespective of differences of faith or race or nation
or habit or opinion or kingdom of nature, there do
we see individualities definitely approaching the kingship to be found at the summit of the human kingdom;
and we may be sure that those who are super-human
are giving them what help they are capable of receiving.

Theosophy also states that these super-human pers-
onages form a Company, a Brotherhood, organized to
direct and guide the world's evolution along the
shortest pathway to its goal.

It is impossible, within the compass of this book,
to set forth the extraordinarily fascinating vistas
which Theosophy discloses in this particular department. But other books describe the Elder Brethren,
as we may call them, their splendid work, and the
way in which we may draw near to them and even
help them.

CHAPTER V

YOUR CIRCUMSTANCES AND SURROUNDINGS

YOUR circumstances are self-made. That is the supreme truth to be realized when you observe your conditions of life. There is no such thing as chance or luck. There is only law. And though we think we see anything but Law, the truth is that we see nothing but Law, for Law is there even though we cannot see it.

We see everywhere inequality, both of condition and of opportunity.

We see favourable surroundings and unfavourable surroundings.

We see individuals able to make much even of a little, and we see individuals unable to make anything even of a wealth of opportunity.

We see individuals born fortunately and happily, with lives before them of ease and joy. We see individuals born amidst conditions of great misery, with only the blackest of prospects awaiting them.

We see individuals born handicapped from the very beginning by disease, by feeble-mindedness, by criminal propensities, by uncontrollable passions. We see individuals born with every conceivable circumstance weighted in their favour, so that success is assured to them no matter what they undertake.

We see individuals destined for genius and heroism and sainthood. We see individuals condemned to lead the most ordinary and sordid of lives.

We see individuals soaring to power. We see individuals submerged in slavery.

We see around us beautiful forms and ugly forms, generous hearts and selfish hearts, intelligent minds and stupid minds, refined natures and crude natures.

Everywhere inequality, and inevitably so, because each one of us is at his own particular stage of unfoldment, no one at exactly the same stage as anyone else.

But whatever the circumstance may be, it is self-made. As we have lived in previous births so are we today. As we have sown in lives gone by, so are we reaping today. As our needs will be for tomorrow and for innumerable tomorrows, so are we sowing and fashioning today. The law of nature or life is such that each individual, says Theosophy, has just the surroundings appropriate to his stage of unfoldment, and the fact that more or less the same surroundings are common to a number of us merely shows that a number of us are more or less, though by no means quite, the same. And each one of us, however common the surroundings may be, reacts, in some measure at least, differently to them.

But it is not enough to say that we have the surroundings which are appropriate to our various stages of evolution. As I have already said, we must also realize that in these surroundings lies what we need in order to take the next step on our unfolding way. Thus, our surroundings and circumstances have a twofold function. They express our stage of development, and they contain the materials necessary for our further building. They are fulfilments and opportunities.

You are born poor because you have invested, in one way or in another, in poverty. But your very poverty contains that power wherewith you shall overcome poverty. You are born with some incurable disease because you have invested in it, in some way or another. It is a natural and inevitable consequence of some activity in the past. But it is as much a blessing as it appears to be a curse. There are other ways of triumphing over it than that of getting rid of it, which, since we assume it is incurable, you will be unable to do.

You are born in the midst of the most hopeless circumstances, because, for the time being, these are appropriate to your stage of evolution. But they are also appropriate to your need for escape and release from them.

You are born with poor intelligence, friendless, unwanted, uncared for, thwarted at every turn. It is the law, your law, You. You alone can change yourself, and thus change your surroundings which are but extensions of yourself. And you will change yourself, sooner or later—the sooner, the more you know; the later, the less you know.

This view of life and of life's circumstances is in fact extraordinarily encouraging, because it sets the eternal " I " against all fleeting circumstances, and shows that victory must be to eternity and not to time. It shows that no surroundings, however overwhelming in devastating power they may appear to be, are more potent in the long run than that which created them. The " I " can modify that which he has made. And Theosophy invokes the " I " to know himself and to hasten on his way to Kingship. Theosophy is more concerned with awakening the " I " than with changing his surroundings. For the moment he is really awake, and knows himself for what he is, he will himself change his surroundings, gradually mastering them, and will pass onwards and onwards from freedom to freedom.

The myriads of " I's ", as they are, are the cause of the world as it is. To modify the effect, the cause itself must change. And while, in the name of the all-embracing unity of life, philanthropic " I's " must strive to eliminate the ugly in all surroundings, in the long run it is only the individual " I " who can make any improvement deep and lasting. Surely must we be active in good work in the outer world, helping our brethren to the utmost in every kingdom of nature. But even more active should we be in helping the " I's " around us to know themselves, and to live their own individual lives more perfectly.

Each one of us can help from without, for such help is an expression of the truth that we are brothers in a common adventure. But our best help is to help an " I " to help himself.

It is, therefore, foolish to inveigh against so-called " fact ", against so-called " injustice ", against inequality, against the fact that others have that which is denied to us. Each of us is his own fate. He makes it, he must bear it, he must profit from it, until it becomes so splendid that he calls it favour.

At the earliest possible moment the individual should be helped to understand that he has equipped himself with what he has and is. He should be encouraged to take stock of his assets and liabilities, of his credits and debits, to strive to increase the former and minimize the latter, transmuting them into that which essentially they are—power, even though they seem but poverty. He should be encouraged to look upon himself as a business man, the head of a working concern. He has credits, he has merchandise in the shape of faculties, he has debts in the shape of weaknesses, and doubtless also in the shape of liabilities to individuals around him whom in previous lives he may have treated in an " unbusiness-like " manner. He must not waste time worrying over his debts. He must not be so full of thought of them that he has no energy left to make use of his credits —few though these may possibly be. He may feel himself to be down, but Theosophy tells him, most emphatically, that he never is, and never can be, out.

He is the head of his business. His various states of consciousness—emotions, mind, physical body—are his partners and stock in trade, and also, of course, his liabilities. His surroundings are the conditions in which he has elected to do his business, knowing that he can make a better profit out of them than out of any other surroundings, strange and even doubtful though the statement may seem. We often cry out: If only I had other surroundings, if only I had what I have not! Futile and ignorant cry! What we have is our best opportunity, for it helps us to achieve that which we have not, and it is because we do not yet know this truth that so often we remain our surroundings' slaves, impotent and resentful.

What we have is the summation of what we have had, and the seed of that which is yet to come. It is all grain. There is no chaff but grain in wrong perspective.

The home in which you live with your family, the circumstances of the family life, the relations between yourself and the other members of your family, the furniture and other appurtenances of the dwelling, the street in which your house is situated, the district in which you live, the occupations in which your relatives and possibly you yourself are engaged, the school or college you may attend, the amusements in which you indulge, the restrictions which you are forced to practise, the circle of friends which surrounds you, the domestic peace and storm which alternate, the ailments, the pre-occupations of many kinds which give you food for thought, the hopes, the anxieties, the joys, the sorrows, the aspirations, the good intentions: all these are part of *you*, are your *mise-en-scène* for the new birth in the midst of which you find yourself.

You have been leading up to them for centuries, even for millenia. Neither Rome nor Kingship was built in a day. You have not become what you are in a moment. The details of your everyday living do not just flash into existence from one moment to the next. Each is part of a long and steady sequence, determined as to its present nature from long ago. It is, however simple it may look, the complex effect of a conglomeration of multitudinous causes.

Lest this should give an impression of helplessness and impotence, of a fly hopelessly struggling in the web of the spider of grim determination, let Theosophy point out to you that nothing whatever is unalterably settled, partly because you can, here and now, substantially modify that which comes upon you from out of the past, and partly because the future, strange to say, has its own influence upon the present no less powerful than that of the past. Clouds may have come up, or may be coming up, from that west which we call the past. But the sun is shining upon us from a future which we may call the east. And he is shining even though we cannot always see him, even though we interpose, between ourselves and him, the cloud-barriers of our ignorance. The past must reckon with the present. The past must also reckon with the future. The more we know about the future, and the more we become able, through the magic of wisdom, to live in the future as well as in the present, the more will it be possible for us to lessen any cold blasts from the past by confronting them with the powerful rays of the glorious sun of the future.

We cannot prevent causes from giving rise to effects, but we can modify the causes by adding to them. So do we modify the effects.

When we realize this truth, the past will be as an open book to us, for we shall have utterly lost all fear of it. We shall know all about our past births. We shall know what is coming to us both of sunshine and of storm. But while we still remain afraid of the past, not knowing we are its masters, it is mercifully hidden from us, and so effectively that we have come to believe that there is no past. Where ignorance seems, and doubtless is, safety, it may be premature to be wise. But as births come and go, courage increases until the traveller insists upon knowing, willing to face all for the sake of knowledge. Then are the veils of ignorance rent asunder. He knows the past, is courageous in the present, and glories in the future.

Let us now look at some special media for the growing individual. Take religion.

An individual is born into a religion partly because the religion suits him, and partly also because he needs it. The religion to which he happens to belong is in its own way a reflection of Truth, a ray constitutive of the great White Light. There are other religions. They, too, are rays from the same source, and are appropriate to the needs of those who belong to them. Every religion is a class in the great school of life, has its own curriculum, its own methods, its own special principles. When an individual takes a new birth he generally joins one or another of these classes, and is educated in the teaching belonging to the class he has joined.

If he be still young in the human stage of his evolutionary process, he will probably insist that his particular class is better than all other classes, in fact that his own class is the only real class, all others being spurious and giving no true teaching at all.

Very young children often point to their own particular toys as being far, far better than those belonging to their little friends. They will tell you that their parents are much better parents than the parents of their comrades. They will tell you of the splendours of their possessions, and how marvellous these are compared with the worthless possessions, of other families. How proud we are of what we have! As if we had been singled out for unique and priceless favours. How we do like to feel we are different, more fortunate, nearer to Truth, than others! And we actually believe that such pride, with an admixture of the sense of security and special protection, is nothing less than truth!

Theosophy takes the conceit out of us, and helps us to realize that we are all much-of-a-muchness, each with his own advantages, each with his own disadvantages. Theosophy cuts at the very root of that ignorant sense of superiority which causes an individual belonging to one religion to have no doubt that he has the truth and that others who do not belong to his faith have, at the best, camouflaged falsehood. Theosophy tells us that we are born into a religion in order to profit from the truths it holds, that we need the truths it holds, even though the time may come when we shall shake ourselves free from its forms because we are able to penetrate below the surface it presents to the world at large.

Religion is only transcended when an individual is at home in all religions. From one point of view religions may indeed be prisons, but unless we learn the lesson of beating against what look like prison bars we are not ready to profit from the open spaces beyond. And when we have learned the lesson, we see that, in fact, there are no bars at all, just opportunities. So we move freely within and without any and every religion—at home in them all and outside them all, restricted by none, free in the colour of each, strong in the white light of them all.

When we describe conditions as barriers or prisons we have failed to understand their nature, we have not yet understood them. In fact they still confine us. The individual who denounces religion, or ceremony, or conviction, or that which to another is truth, has still to learn the lessons these teach, and that all need to learn. He has escaped from them, or thinks he has, too soon. In this world there is nothing but opportunity, even though we may no longer need some opportunities. The wise man is he who can dwell freely everywhere, in religion, out of religion, in ceremony, out of ceremony, in nationality, out of nationality, in forms, outside forms, in narrowness, outside narrowness. The wise man is free of all life, and rejoices in it. The wise man knows no limitations to his kingship, no prisons, no bars. Everywhere he is king, and lives everywhere royally.

Let us finally consider nationality.

The principle is identical with that which underlies religion. An individual is born into a nation because he needs to learn the lessons that nation has to teach —each nation being another type of class in the great world-school. He must not forget the less under the glamour of the more. He must not forget all he has to learn from membership of the nation-class while contemplating the grandeur of the great world-school.

Internationalism is composed of a number of national ingredients and to leave out any particular ingredient vitiates the whole of which they are essential parts. We must learn to be finely national, so that we may the sooner become finely international. We must learn to contribute to the international whole a beautiful national part. We must be full of the national spirit —full, that is, of patriotism, a patriotism dedicated to a smaller brotherhood, itself strong and harmonious, and contributing its strength to a larger brotherhood. The White Light cannot live without its component colours; without them it would be no White Light. Similarly, internationalism is not true internationalism if any of its national ingredients are left out.

We must be earnest, eager students in our religion, nation, and race classes. We must be proud of these classes because of the truths they hold for our unfoldment. We must become able more and more to rejoice in the depths of the wisdom of which they are custodians. Generally, if we cease to be able to perceive truth in any one of these classes it is because our eyes are not yet strong enough to see, beyond the surfaces, into those depths which ordinarily are hidden from the ken of those who still belong to surfaces alone.

CHAPTER VI

YOUR BUSINESS AND YOUR LEISURE

IT might be thought that Theosophy would have little to say as to an individual's ways of earning his living, or as to the way in which an individual should enjoy his leisure hours. Yet Theosophy has much to say about both.

Theosophy looks upon an individual as an evolving unity—evolving both on his own individual account and as a cell or organism in the great body of evolving nature. This is one of Theosophy's great principles. Theosophy envisages every single attitude and every single activity of the individual as an integral part of the universal evolutionary process, so that his aspirations, his ideals, his hopes, his emotions and feelings, his occupations, all are part of the evolutionary process at work. They are the evolutionary process at work in the twofold and simultaneous process of moving him, and at the same time the whole of life, upon the unfolding way.

What profession does the individual choose? The choice, and its resulting release of specialized force, is latent with power for growth, and that which is latent gradually becomes definitely patent, whether the choice, from the point of view of the outer world, turns out ill or well.

Even if the choice turn out badly, the experience of apparent failure contains within itself compensations for the failure. There is not a single experience upon which we shall not, sooner or later, look back with satisfaction, however devastating it may have seemed to be at the time. There is not a single experience with regard to which we shall not say: " Well, terrible though it was, depressing setback though it seemed to be, and perhaps was, at the time, still I would not be without it, if for no other reason than that it enables me to sympathize intimately with those who are going through the same sort of experience."

Let us then look, from the Theosophical point of view, at a number of choices, and not trouble very much about the way in which they turn out, except to remind ourselves that all is grist which comes to the mills of growth.

Theosophy looks upon a profession or business as a step in the direction of self-realization, both for the individual self and no less for the collective self.

Hence, no matter what the nature of the profession or business, it is an opportunity for service by the individual who is engaged in it, to himself, to his community, and to the world as a whole.

Certain special types of service are, in the light of Theosophy, outstanding. There is the service of the statesman, the priest, the teacher. There is the service of the soldier—the defender. There is the service of the ruler. There is the service of the merchant, the industrialist, the individual engaged in commerce. There is the service of the worker who has not specialized in any particular profession. There is the service of the artist, the musician, the sculptor, the philosopher, the architect, the actor.

Theosophy sees each of these services as a channel of offering to the community as well as a means of livelihood. The acid test as to whether wise use is being made of business or profession is the extent to which the individual is able to combine a happy and a due distribution of the fruits of his work between his individual self and the collective self of which he forms part.

He is surely right to spend part of his earnings on comforts as well as on necessities, so that he may live restfully and aspiringly. But he has a duty to the community no less insistent than his duty to himself; and neither duty is accomplished unless the other duty is also fulfilled. Much of the depression is the result of a concentration on the individual self at the expense of the collective self. They grow together or not at all.

Were the world's educational systems equal to their duty, the earlier years of a young citizen's life would serve to indicate, with exactitude, the nature of the profession most suitable to his temperament; and during the later part of his educational life he would receive training in that profession. A nation, Theosophically organized, would have a very clear realization of the priceless asset to its prosperity of every young life born and growing up as an integral part of its organism.

There would, therefore, be no criminal wastage of life, such as we see when a nation's youthful citizens seek in vain for employment, for an outlet for their young and enthusiastic energies. A nation Theosophically organized would perceive clearly that it could not possibly afford to lose a single unit of vibrant citizen-power, specially at the time when this power is in its budding strength. A Theosophical government would regard as a special duty the harnessing of its youth to the service of the nation. There would be a job waiting for every citizen on the attainment of his majority, though there would be no interference with any arrangements, privately made, for employment.

At the present moment life is composed largely of misfits, even though these misfits are not in fact as destructive as often they appear; for the very misfit has its constructive values and purpose. Citizens who ought to be in one profession, in one particular type of service, are languishing in another, to the detriment of their own growth and of the well-being of the nation. Culture suffers to an almost inconceivable degree from the fact that those who in special measure minister to it—the artists, musicians, sculptors, actors and architects—are for the most part left to fend for themselves, the nation failing to understand that upon such as these its real life depends. A nation is said to perish where there is no vision. It perishes no less where there is no effective appreciation and encouragement of culture.

The fundamental principles common to all business, to all professions, are honesty, dignity, efficiency, and service. Indeed, from a Theosophical standpoint, the education of these qualities is the *raison d'être* of business and profession. And, from the Theosophical point of view, there is no distinction whatever between manual and any other kind of work. There is as much true worth in work that is handwork, of whatever kind, as in work that is brainwork. Character is fed as richly by the hand as it is by mind and emotions. And the handwork which brings the individual very near to nature, to mother earth, is supremely character-forming.

The time should come when people will cease to herd together in large cities, far away from the earth which is so truly their mother, and will return to the land which, from one point of view, they need never have left. " Back to the land " contains, Theosophically speaking, a very deep truth. To live near to nature, to be content with natural enjoyments, to return to simplicity and peace: these, far from being inconsistent with growth, are in fact growth's greatest stimuli.

If our educational systems were truer, less artificial, less ignorant, many young citizens, both boys and girls, would be educated to find their satisfactions and their livelihoods in natural modes of living, to be content with simple pleasures, and to find in communion with nature ample food for the needs of the body, the emotions and the mind. Books, constant association with other people, the artificial stimulation of mental and emotional appetites by our so-called civilization—all these are by no means as vitally necessary as we are brought up to think. We have made life extraordinarily complex when its goal is simplicity. We crave for sensation, and the bizarre has even entered the sacred precincts of Art, so that in the very name of art we find men and women distorting beauty and simplicity out of all recognition. Just as in the French Revolution the goddess of reason replaced the great progenitor of the Christian faith, so today ugliness has in a measure dethroned grace and reigns in its name.

There need be, there must be, no ugliness, no sordidness, in business. We are often told that business is a dirty game. It is we who make it dirty. In reality business is a splendidly clean game, a game in which each player himself grows and helps his fellow players to grow. Let us beware of imagining that we are unfortunate in having to devote most of our time to business when we would fain occupy ourselves with matters seemingly more spiritual and more helpful to our fellow men. It is a terrible mistake to believe that we are doing good only when we are preaching good, or when we are engaged in some kind of philanthropic activity. How many good people are constantly wishing they could be free from the necessity of earning their livelihood, so that they might devote themselves to service! As if the earning of a livelihood is not as much service as that which, too often, begins and ends on the public platform. As if honourable business is not as fine a contribution to the community as time spent in emotional exhortations, and in asking other people to contribute money to " good causes ".

We must learn to exalt business, to exalt the professions, to dignify labour; and not to be led away by the assertion that if one desires to be successful in business it is impossible to lead an honest life. Are there no men of honour in business or in the

professions? Is the whole of our business and pro-
fessional life corrupt? Evidence is all to the contrary,
though it may be by no means untrue that some
people who are in business, especially those who
belong to the get-rich-quick fraternity, do not know
how to combine honour with success.

And now as to leisure.

There is in business an inevitable discipline and
self-control. In business a definite goal is being
pursued, and the business man realizes that without
discipline and self-control he cannot reach that goal.
Leisure is in a way just as much a business as is
business itself. It is a mode of growth, as business
is. But it takes the special form of recreation through
relaxation, or through the diverting of the attention
from that which normally occupies and indeed pre-
occupies it.

The essential characteristics of true and constructive
leisure are happiness and refinement. In all leisure
there should be a sense of light-heartedness and an
absence of vulgarity, more particularly as regards the
most beautiful and sacred thing in life—the relation
between man and woman. It is much to be deplored
that newspapers, books, theatres and picture-houses,
often cater recklessly to sensation, to passion, to
licence.

Intent on selfish and destructive living, indifferent
to the evil they work upon the community, and
especially upon its younger members, many editors
and proprietors of newspapers, many authors of
books, many proprietors of theatres and picture-
houses and producers of films, day after day callously

stimulate the vulgar, the sordid, the sensational, show indifference to law and order, and to all reverence for the human form. They declare that they must live, and that the public must be given what it wants.

One feels inclined to repeat, as regards the first assertion, that cruel and untrue utterance of Talleyrand: *Je ne vois pas la necessité*. Of course they must live, but they might surely live as civilized human beings and not as savages, standing in the way of the process of evolution, hindering it, setting themselves up against it. Nemesis will sooner or later overtake them, for as we sow so must we reap. But since Nemesis often pauses to let men have their fling, so that they may learn their lesson the more surely, it sometimes seems as if there were no Nemesis at all, no certainty of cause being followed by effect. It is not difficult to read, in the faces of those who indulge in such so-called leisure, the writing of these enemies of all that is wonderful and glorious in life, and in the forms of life. And as for the allegation that the public must be given what it wants, is it not true that the public is generally taught to want what it is given?

The creative and happy use of leisure is one of the great objects both of education and of all other means whereby the life in us is released from sleep to sparkling wakefulness.

Leisure should be used to the end of grace and hardihood of body, of simplicity and regularity in food and habits. The body should be at the extreme neither of over-development nor of under-development. There is distortion and crudity in either. The body should be trained to be a thoroughly reliable servant, never a peevish tyrant.

Leisure should be used to the end of stimulating all higher emotions and feelings, and of starving the lower. Appreciation of the beautiful, joy in aspiration, happiness in service, delight in the noble, a reverent use of the creative forces, tenderness for weakness and ignorance—to such ends alone should leisure be dedicated.

Leisure should be used to stimulate the mind to accord with the noblest conceptions of life: in some measure at least to plumb compassionately the depths of man's unhappiness and reverently to sense the heights reached by the flowers of earth's humanity: to revel in great vistas of unfoldment: and unerringly to use discrimination to distinguish between that which, for the particular mind concerned, is true and right and that which is untrue and wrong, because no longer expedient for growth. Is not the conception of right and wrong entirely relative, based on the very real principle enshrined in the adage that while one man's meat is another man's poison, one man's poison may well be another man's meat, and probably is?

Theosophy emphatically declares that just as everywhere is opportunity, so everything is truth—absolutely on its own plane, relatively, down here. Hence, each mind, in discriminating between right and wrong, should add the pregnant words: FOR ME.

Leisure should also be used for awakening those higher states of consciousness which, in the majority of mankind, are still asleep, or but just beginning to stir. Theosophy tells us of a number of states of consciousness from the physical right up to very lofty regions of which the vast majority of us have no experience whatever. In meditation, in contemplation, in aspiration, such states may sometimes be touched and their glories to a small degree perceived. In ecstasies and in visions they may even be experienced, though they cannot be understood, and all descriptions of them must inevitably be inaccurate and distorted by the personal equation of the experimenter. Leisure may indeed be well employed in occasional withdrawals from the all-too-familiar states of consciousness in which we normally live and move and have our being; in occasional ascents to individuality's peaks within, to know, in their silence and power, that Life is indeed One and that Individuality is limitless in its stupendous potencies.

Your business may be the body of life, but leisure is surely life's soul. And Theosophy will add that in truth body and soul are one. The body is the mirror of the soul, and the soul is the apotheosis of the body.

CHAPTER VII

YOUR WORLD IN PEACE AND WAR

WE have the strangest notions as to the nature of war and of peace. Practically, we restrict these two words to armed conflict, or the absence of it, between one country and another. When there is no actual physical fighting we say there is peace. When such fighting is in progress we say there is war.

Constantly we are praying for peace in our time, and while we are praying we are fighting, or we are planning to fight.

Theosophy goes very searchingly into the whole question of peace and war, and begins by declaring that what we call war is but the last outward and visible sign of a number of preceding conditions in other states of consciousness, as high up, it may be, as the mind. A state of physical war is war which has already been existing elsewhere, only finding its ultimate expression on the physical plane.

The murder of the Austrian archduke was in fact a remote cause of the first world war. It was but one of a number of inevitable alternatives consequent on war already at work in other states of consciousness. And when the word *war* is used it is a synonym for *hatred*. There is no war but hatred: not by any means necessarily hatred in those who are taking part in physical plane war, in all probability on the contrary; but certainly hatred among those who have been thinking and feeling in terms of war.

War takes root in mental and emotional conditions, and only at last finds its way down to the physical plane in some event precipitated by a converging of mental and emotional intensities.

Further, Theosophy is emphatic in declaring that war is by no means to be regarded as exclusively a matter of the human race. The war spirit is abroad in humanity, setting one section against another. War is abroad between humanity and the kingdoms of nature below the human. Humanity is constantly fighting the animal kingdom, the vegetable kingdom, the mineral kingdom. These kingdoms, too, are engaged in internal warfare, and in war as between one kingdom and another.

The war spirit is abroad because the war spirit has its place and purpose and power in the evolutionary process, at all events up to a certain point. The most pronounced pacifist may declare that he abhors war, and will do nothing to promote it. He will be a wonderful conscientious objector, and suffer all manner of pains and penalties for the sake of his conscience. Yet he may be as contributory to war as the most fiery fighter, for his conscience may only see a very little way.

If he be an eater of flesh, a wearer of furs, a vivisector, a participator in the hunting of animals, or in any other way uses his might against weakness and the right of weakness, he is taking part in war— war against his younger fellow-members of the universal family.

He may justify the war spirit in himself. He may invoke the false law of the survival of the fittest. He may point out that nobody, with any sense, would regard the eating of meat as an exhibition of the war spirit—"the idea is ridiculous, absurd, just the sort of notion one would expect from one of these un-balanced fanatics." He may be sure he is right. Yet he is, in cold, hard fact, a war-monger; for while he may abhor one kind of war, denounce it, be quite rabid about it, he is hard at work promoting another kind of war—and there will be people as rabid about his war spirit as he is rabid about the war spirit of people who do not condemn war among humans as he condemns it.

The war spirit is essentially one and indivisible, however it be expressed. We may denounce it as expressed in one form and take part in it when in another form. But as we vitalize it in one direction it becomes increasingly potent in all directions.

Theosophy does not condemn the war spirit lock, stock and barrel. Theosophy recognizes that the war spirit is an evolutionary stage. It has its work to do, and it will not disappear until its work is done. It will not disappear until the spirit of war ceases to exist altogether. It will not disappear, so far as the human kingdom is concerned, until humanity has learned to transcend it, not only within its own kingdom, but no less in humanity's relations to all other kingdoms. So long as humanity, as a whole, is at war with the sub-human kingdoms of nature, so long is it fostering war within its own ranks.

The world wars, for example, may be immediately traced to human causes. To what extent was each war the expression of the pent-up spirit of war generated through centuries by the constant warring against kingdoms of nature helpless to retaliate? The spirit of war recoils upon its possessor, as the boomerang returns to the thrower. Sent forth against other kingdoms, it returns to work havoc in the human kingdom.

It may be argued that the first work incumbent upon members of the human kingdom is to get rid of war in their own midst, that when human wars are no more it will be time enough to abolish other wars. In fact, however, a League to abolish war between the human and the animal kingdoms, an inter-Kingdom war, is far more important than a League to abolish inter-human war. The latter, at least, is more or less a war among equals, among those who can, more or less, fight back. There may be some honour, some dignity, some self-respect, in such a war. But war in which one side is practically omnipotent and the other side practically impotent is no war at all, it is just massacre, just the pitting of mental cunning against weak ignorance.

No League to abolish war within the human kingdom stands the slightest chance of success unless and until, as a pure matter of logic, it includes war between the human and the lower kingdoms. Something may be better than nothing, and it may be better to have a League with restricted objective rather than no League at all. True, but let us not fondly imagine that war is going to cease until the will to war, in any form, has disappeared from the hearts of men. Orthodoxy, conventionality, that which passes in these days for reason and common sense —all are for the maintenance of the war spirit in one form or in another. Only when the world of human beings begins to see more clearly, to reason more accurately, and to make common some of that sense which for the time being is unfortunately so uncommon, will wars between nations and peoples come to a close.

What are the ingredients of the war spirit? There are in fact many. Hatred ranks high, of course, and specially that so-called righteous hatred which justifies its venom. The inquisitions of the Middle Ages were examples of such hatred. And it still survives, though no longer so much in evidence on the physical plane in the torturing of the physical body. We have discovered subtler methods of torture with advancing " civilization "!

In many departments of life hatred still has its prominent place. There is hatred between people of different political persuasions. There is hatred be- tween people of different religious persuasions, even within a single faith. There is hatred between people of different nationalities, of different races. There is hatred between people of different opinions and habits. There is widespread suspicion and distrust—the precursors of hatred.

Instead of understanding and appreciation, there is pride and its concomitant, a sense of superiority, and it is not a very long way from pride to hatred. We thus find in pride and its permutations and combinations another ingredient of the war spirit. Pride of race, pride of nationality, pride of faith, pride of place, pride of power—these are indeed powerful aids to the propagation and intensification of the war spirit. And their potency becomes all the more irresistible when they are permeated by the spirit of self-righteousness and mis-named duty. How much hatred is generated, on the one side by those whose sense of superiority tramples underfoot alleged inferiors, and on the other side by those who are compelled to suffer the trampling without means of retaliation. There may be upper-dogs and under-dogs. But very often there is little to choose between them as regards the measure of their mutual hatred. Is there much to choose between extremes? Both parties worship at the altar of hatred, and sooner or later the god of hatred will answer the prayers of all his worshippers and cause devastation among them.

Pride is also present in those who are bitterly opposed to pride of race, of nationality, of faith, of place, of power.

But the vital ingredient in the war spirit is ignorance. Wherever there is hatred there is ignorance. Wherever there is pride there is ignorance. Wherever there is oppression, a sense of superiority, injustice, tyranny, there is ignorance. Wherever there is the prostitution of weakness, in no matter what kingdom of nature, to the greed of strength, there is ignorance. Ignorance is the progenitor of hatred and of all war. And unless we learn to perceive ignorance in its ugly effects we shall have no incentive to become wise. Therefore is it that Theosophy is able to perceive the place of the war spirit, of war, and even of hatred and its concomitants, in the educative process of life's unfolding nature. Only as ignorance disappears will war disappear. Only as war disappears everywhere will war disappear anywhere, though, paradoxically, it is no less true that only as war disappears somewhere will it disappear everywhere.

If the question be asked: Has the world finished with war? Was the last war a war to end war? the answer, from the Theosophical standpoint, is without the slightest element of doubt, that the world has *not* finished with war. The last war, though it should have been a war to end war, had humanity understood the lesson thoroughly, has, as we are able to perceive so clearly today, by no means driven home its ghastly lesson. Is the war spirit in one of its innumerable forms no longer abroad? Have we sheathed the sword, so that there is not even the whisper of war between nation and nation, creed and creed, prejudice and prejudice? Have the raids on the animal kingdom ceased, so that we no longer terrify them for sport, agonise them for adornment, kill them to satisfy our appetites? Do we no longer deface the country side with hideous advertisements of valueless inventions, wantonly spread death among trees and flowers in order to pander to our conveniences and our tastes, make hideous beautiful nature by defiling her with nightmare buildings? Have we done with imprisoning the life in the mineral kingdom in forms of ugliness which we condone as utilitarian?

The war spirit is at fever heat everywhere, and we think we are doing away with it entirely by trying to do away with part of it!

Humanity cannot escape war in its midst while it spreads war among those younger members of the universal family for whom, as the elder brother, it has both a moral and a spiritual responsibility. War is the nemesis for injustice, for cruelty, for tyranny. And while these forms of ignorance last, war will continue, nation will be arrayed against nation, faith against faith, individual against individual.

But it is of the highest importance to make clear that Theosophy neither sits in judgment upon people, nor preaches in a spirit of dogmatism. It utters no words of condemnation, still less words of damnation. Theosophy declares Truth, but leaves people free to take what they can of it, and to leave what they will. We perceive Truth in accordance with the stage of diminishing ignorance which we happen to have reached, and there is no more fault to be found with an individual because he is unable to accept a particular truth than with a child for not being older than he is.

Lest much of the above, therefore, appear dogmatic and highly controversial, let it be stated that everything set forth in this, or in any other chapter, is in the first place an individual understanding of the Truths of Theosophy, and must needs be partial and coloured by the personal equation. In the second place, it is a statement of such Truth as the writer is able to perceive. Thirdly, it is in no way whatever a setting forth of a creed which must be believed if salvation is to be reached.

The writer of this book is only in very small measure able to incarnate some of the truths he has discovered. He does not say: This is how I live. He says rather: This is how I shall probably someday live.

Every reader will take that which is congenial to him, and leave that which is uncongenial, without incurring the judgment that he has been weighed in the balance and found wanting.

Theosophy clearly indicates that everybody is constantly being weighed in the balance and is never found wanting, save, it may be, for a little while. Nobody is in danger of missing salvation, for the simple reason that we are being saved all the time, though sometimes to a greater and sometimes to a lesser degree.

Salvation is the heart of time, for time exists to make sure that we shall all attain salvation—howsoever the word may be defined. Each moment of time is drawing us slowly but surely, though often to human gaze invisibly, nearer and nearer to salvation. Hence, looking at all the assertions made, for example, in this chapter, not one single one of them is to be taken as an acid test of righteousness. No one can, Theosophically speaking, be looked down upon because he does not follow this or that exhortation. Theosophy leaves us all free, and is instinct with the truth that in all probability each one of us is moving towards his journey's end as rapidly as he can.

Yet the Truths remain, whatever may be the judgment we pass upon them. And there is nothing better for us, nothing more truly exhilarating and stimulating to the determined seeker after truth, than

the setting before our eyes of Truths which have
existed from the beginning of time, and are the very
breath of life.

We may all be thanking God we are not as others
are.   But those very others may be far nearer the goal
than our sanctimonious and self-satisfied selves.   And
if we are fanatics, reformers, and the like—it is very
good for some of us, though it would be very bad for
all of us, to be of these persuasions—we must indeed
beware of the ugly and disastrous conceit that those
who are not for us are against Truth.   They may
possibly be against a fragment of the truth which we
are, very imperfectly, seeing; but they may be for a
fragment of the truth which we cannot see at all, a
larger fragment, possibly, than that which we ourselves
possess, and of which we are so absurdly proud.

"A" may be a vegetarian and one who does not
indulge in hunting for so-called "sport".   He may
be very sad that "B" is so far undeveloped that he
remains a meat-eater and hunts.   "A" may carry on
the most intense campaign in the most ardent language
against "these horrible cruelties" declaring there is
little hope for the future until they cease to be
practised.   And he will be perfectly right.   On the
other hand "B" may, in fact, be a far finer person
than "A", nobler in a number of ways, and may be
practising truths of which "A" has yet to gain
conception.

Our business is to stand strongly for principles, but
never to attack persons, about whose lives we can
know but little.   The identification of persons with
the evils we attack is one of the most fruitful sources

of that discord which so often ends in war. Most of us are so very personal that half the satisfaction of fighting disappears if there be not somebody to attack.

Fortunately, Theosophy is not a creed, still less a dogma or a doctrine. Neither is it an orthodoxy, nor an acid test of rectitude. Theosophy is the Science of Life, impersonal, unjudging, non-critical. Each of its votaries takes that which he can understand, practises that which is congenial to him, at his own particular stage of evolution. That which he does not understand he leaves alone, for the time being. He is not so foolish as to deny it. And there are no distinctions between the votaries because one accepts this and another accepts that.

In war we see the outward and visible sign of the ignorance which we are in process of replacing by wisdom. Since ignorance takes time to pass away, war must also take time to pass away.

Peace is the outward and visible sign of wisdom. Where peace is not, wisdom is less. Where peace is, there wisdom has taken the place of ignorance. And let us disabuse ourselves of the superstition that ignorance can ever be bliss, so that sometimes it may be folly to be wise. It can never be folly to be wise, for wisdom alone is bliss, and ignorance alone can be folly.

CHAPTER VIII

YOU AND DECISION-MAKING

THEOSOPHY is wonderfully useful in helping you to make up your mind—a feat which quite a number of people find not a little difficult.

Theosophy tells you, for example, that when you do happen to make it up you are, in all probability, not only making up your mind but also your emotions, for emotions are even weightier and more constant than the mind in the influence they exercise over prospective decisions.

Theosophy further declares that when you are making up mind and emotions, which is another way, for most of us, of saying 'giving them more or less free play', the background of your past, the point of your present, and the shadows of your future, become the determining factors. Up to a certain point your decision is already taken, but unless it so happens that there are influences at work too strong to be affected either by present or by future, you will be able to modify that decision substantially, even divert it altogether from its normal direction. In addition to the mind and the emotions, and all those forces which have been set in motion, perhaps from a very long time back—in addition to all these which are ever hard at work 'making you up', there is also

that will which is the most accurate reflection of your
eternal self available for use in this outer world.

Few people make much use of their wills. Most of
us are content to be shuttlecocks battledored through
life by the circumstances which come up against us,
and by the fleeting thoughts and emotions which from
time to time float through our consciousness. We are
children of the wind, or shall we say, less pictures-
quely, straws blown hither and thither by the varying
winds of life. We live from below, largely perhaps,
because we do not know any above.

But Theosophy lays the very greatest stress on the
above, pointing out that the above is only waiting the
opportunity, so frequently denied to it by the below,
of taking part in the life below and of proving a most
valuable adviser; and, even more, a force which will
soon be realized as comparatively infallible in all its
judgments. In fact, says the " above ", the " below "
will some day be saying: " I cannot imagine how I
was able for so long to do without that ' above '
which now I am so thankful to have taken into
partnership."

The will is this " above ", not the so-called will which
is often nothing more than kaleidoscopically changing
impulse, but the will embodying that spark of life itself
whose pilgrimage through the stage of flame to that
of fire we watch in the interplay of individuality and
surroundings.

We might, indeed, suggest that not only must mind
and emotions be made up, but also will, were it not
for the fact that the will has been made up from time
immemorial, and that the object of the making up of

mind and emotions is to submit to the determination of the will the kingdoms of mind and emotions, so turbulently populated in their earlier stages of evolution. The mind must be made up to reflect the inner kingship of the will. Similarly, the emotions must be made up to reflect the inner kingship of the will. Then alone, when General Mind and General Emotions have conquered their respective territories for their Lord, will he, King Will, make his triumphal progress through his new dominions, though he will ever do his best to make himself felt, even while these territories remain unsubdued.

When a decision has to be taken, and mind and emotions have to be made up, it is eminently desirable to try to ascertain the intentions of the will, or higher self.

The consultation may be in the form: " What *ought* I to do? " But this form of question not only gives an air of unreality to the reference, but also suggests that there are two conflicting possibilities of decision—what I ought to do and what I should *like* to do. And often it seems cruel to the persuasive and coaxing " like " to intrude upon it the tiresome and unsympathetic " ought ".

The reference should more accurately be: " What do I *really* want to do? " Let the mind and the emotions by all means be counsellors, insistent counsellors if you will, but they must know their place and keep to it. Give the higher self a hearing. Give the will a chance.

What *does* the real You want? He wants, (sex differentiation does not exist in this larger realm of being), to extend the frontiers of his consciousness, right out to the farthest limits of mind, emotions, and body, so that he may as soon as possible enter upon the full kingship of his life. He knows that these worlds must be conquered, and their wealth garnered for his use. He knows that his agents or generals—the mind-I, the emotions-I, and the body-I —in these outer regions must take time for their conquering of them so as to be sure to miss nothing; that mind, emotions, body must run the gamut of fundamental experiences, though of course they need not sample all in detail. But King Will will be thankful when the harvesting is over and the experiences are at last gathered into his eternal treasure house.

He intends his agents here to be free from fear, for while they are afraid they cannot do their work efficiently for him. He intends his agents to be free from hatred and anger and irritability, for while they are able to hate, and be angry and irritable, they cannot do their work efficiently for him. He intends his agents to be full of enthusiasm, for while they are listless and indifferent they cannot do their work efficiently for him. He intends his agents to be honourable and chivalrous, for aught of dishonour or irreverence renders their work largely infructuous so far as he is concerned. He intends his agents to be full of unquenchable and undiscriminating kindliness and helpfulness, for so long as they are only kind when they feel in the mood and are helpful only in proportion to the return they expect, they cannot do their work efficiently for him.

He intends his agents to be free from separative pride, for while they think themselves superior to other agents, they cannot do their work efficiently for him. He intends his agents to be full of grace and dignity and charm and refinement, for while they remain crude and vulgar and in any way ugly, they cannot do their work efficiently for him.

You see, he wants very much. But he is not unreasonable. He simply asks for that which he knows to be essential to his own happiness, to the happiness of his agents and to the happiness of all. He is only asking for that which he knows he will get, since it is that which his deputies will sooner or later be most happy to give.

Of course, we "I's" down here cannot at once give him all he wants. But it is worth while to know what he wants, so that in making a decision we may see that as far as possible it accords with his needs, which, in very truth, are the real needs of mind, emotions and physical body, if only these "people" could realize the fact. Sooner or later, as I have said, he will get what he wants, but he will not be happy till he gets it, nor shall we, nor the world in any kingdom of its life.

This is one reason why we should remember to ask the will to help us to make decisions, for he is the only member of our "You" family who really does know, quite definitely, what he wants, and who has been wanting the same thing from time immemorial. The rest of the family want one thing now and another thing later on, are constantly ringing the changes on their innumerable wants. But the will, the higher self, knows without the slightest doubt exactly what he wants, consistently asks for the same thing, never grows tired of asking without getting, and will finally get it, for mind and emotions and body will at last find he knows best.

Above all, as expressing the very heart of his purpose, he wants truth. He will not be put off with that which, down here, you may be absolutely certain *is* truth, for he knows that it is only a fragment of truth, and in all probability a very shadowy and distorted fragment.

You may think that your religious principles, your ceremonial observances, a Book, a number of Articles, constitute truth practically unalloyed, and so may they be, for you, down here, at your present stage of evolution. But he knows how poor they are compared with the kind of truth he wants. Hence, however much eminent persons or age-old books may insist that such and such notions are the truth, the whole truth and nothing but the truth, you must hold these notions lightly, for he will not be satisfied until you have changed them almost out of recognition.

You may think that because you no longer belong to a church, no longer participate in ceremonial observances, no longer subscribe to the tenets of the religion to which you once belonged, you have, therefore, escaped from a prison, and are basking in the free air of truth.

You may proudly declare that because you have abandoned a bible, deserted a ceremonial, cut yourself loose from forms, you have, therefore, drawn nearer to truth. You will probably have found an authority who has declared that such abandonment is in the nature of a release from bondage.

Try to remember that the will is cynical—may the word be forgiven—as to the innumerable declarations that such and such alone is freedom and truth, and that at last so and so knows he has achieved truth. How many people are there in the world who continually insist that where you are not, or what you have not, there, or such and such, is truth. And their insistence is based on nothing more than the fact that where they are, and what they have, happens temporarily to be truth for them. We are so extraordinarily conceited that we think far too highly of our own possessions, and far too disparagingly of those possessions of others which are no doubt unsuited to us, though possibly very well suited indeed to them.

We cannot do better than to withdraw, from time to time, from books, from authorities, from persons, from all external utterances, into our highest selves, into the will, that ultimate " I " which sometimes we reach in our most exalted moments. Let us acquire the habit of communing with ourselves at our noblest heights, away from the mind, away from the emotions, away from persons and books, away from heights, soaring, if only momentarily, to the Everests of our eternal being.

Then shall we know what the real " You ", or " I ", wants in relation to any choice, however trivial, which may lie before us, waiting to be submitted to our final Court of Appeal. We shall soon become familiar with the lines of judgment which this Court invariably follows. Are we to do, or to say, or to be, this or that? If we are to satisfy this Court our decision must be permeated by certain qualities, some of which have just been indicated—refinement, dignity, charm, kindliness, courage, honour, efficiency. No choice can possibly finally satisfy the Court if it lacks any one of these qualities.

The mind may be satisfied with less, so may the emotions. They may be satisfied with far, far less— indeed, often with that which negates many of these qualities. Judgment and conscience may fall very short of the Court's requirements. But the will knows, and by constant reference to him, judgment, conscience, mind, emotions, will become exalted; and the time will come when all these shall be for ever one with him.

The will knows. We think we know, often " know " that we know. When, at last, we know that we do not know, then will victory have been won, for then shall we really begin to know.

You may argue that it is ridiculous to go to all this fuss and trouble when the matter to be decided may only be a trivial affair. But the fact is that there is nothing trivial in life, at all. Our idea that some things matter very little, and many not at all, is one of the causes of the difficulties in which we are continually finding ourselves. An apparently little thing comes up for decision. We treat it carelessly, as if it did not much matter whether we decided in one way or in another. And then, as the decision unfolds in its effects, we find ourselves " let in for " conditions and circumstances which we did not dream could possibly be the outcome of such small and trivial beginning. There is nothing small in life. Everything is afire with power to set ablaze a conflagration. A chance word, a petty action, a casual gesture, an entirely unconscious attitude, a thoughtless decision, may well provoke a series of consequences fraught with tremendous effects.

In fact, from the standpoint of Theosophy, even the, apparently, smallest force is the trickle preliminary to a devastating torrent.

Now only the will is really competent to direct these potencies. The mind has its value, of course. So have the emotions their value. But mind and emotions are only partly developed. The will, the higher self, has sent them forth as reflections of himself to gather dominion for him, even to the uttermost limits of manifested life. But they spend much time choosing, desiring, accepting, rejecting, before they become able to give the will exactly what he wants. They themselves have gradually to learn what he wants. You can by no means be sure, therefore, that at any given moment you may rely upon the mind for the best judgment, or upon the emotions for the best desire. Take these two messengers into consultation, but finally refer the problem to the will.

You will say that there is often no time for the deliberateness which such a procedure seems necessarily to involve. Sometimes a decision must be quickly taken, or the opportunity will be lost.

But it takes no time to consult the will. In fact it takes less time to consult the will than to consult mind or emotions, which so frequently, as surely you know, fritter time away in a condition of unstable fluctuation.

If you have not been in the habit of consulting the will in the spirit of: " What do I *really* want to do? ", you may think the process more difficult and less direct than that of putting the question before the mind and emotions. But the extra time you may at first need to take—the time to be taken will diminish in proportion to the frequency of consultation —is a first-class investment, having regard to the fact that your decision is likely to be far wiser and far more productive of lasting happiness and peace.

Of course, the mind and the emotions may tell you that by listening to them you will obtain a quicker return in satisfaction. They will say to you that a bird of satisfaction near to the hand is worth any number of birds of doubtful satisfaction far away in the bush. But the will will reply, if it has the chance, that the bird in the hand is not likely to remain there. It will in all probability fly away. The satisfaction it affords must needs be fleeting. The birds of satisfaction come and go, and the hand cannot forever be stretching itself out to clutch and to abandon alternately. The time must sooner or later come when the hand shall grow tired of seeking, holding, and releasing birds of passage, and shall at last achieve contentment and self-fulfilment in direction from within instead of in allurement from without. Hand happiness derived from without is always fleeting happiness. It is here today and gone tomorrow. But hand happiness derived from joyous co-ordination with the will within is certain to be permanent happiness.

Therefore, whenever you have to make up your mind, try the Theosophical plan of making up your will. It is already much more made up and infinitely more far-sighted than either mind or emotions.

Send up a flash of enquiry, and you will probably receive a flash of response. The will is thankful to be consulted, for the experience is all too rare. You will say: "But must I not use my judgment?" By all means use your judgment, but the judgment is at the most the Court of Appeal.

Theosophy insists that there is something more valuable in us than either judgment or conscience. We may think we have nothing better, but it must be remembered that from the Theosophical point of view both judgment and conscience are mainly the fruit of experience from below. They represent us as far as we have evolved down here in the outer worlds. They are all very well in their way, and certainly we must make good use of them, but there is also that higher Judgment and higher Conscience in the likeness of which the lower judgment and the lower conscience are ever seeking to fashion themselves. There is the Plan which judgment and conscience are seeking to fulfil.

Why not consult the Plan as well as the builders? If we form the habit of consulting the Plan, which is the will, even in the most trivial affairs of everyday life, we shall find both judgment and conscience illumined from above just as they are being steadily built up from below. But not only this. We shall also find that we are beginning to live less in terms of the lower, less exclusively in terms of mind, emotions, body, and more continuously in terms of will and high purpose. We shall begin to live in the eternal, rather than in time, in life rather than in death.

You have a decision to take, in connection with some trivial-seeming matter. If you like, sharpen your judgment and your conscience upon it. These, let us assume, decide: Nihil Obstat. Very well. Now appeal to the higher court—the court of the will. How do you make the appeal? What is the proper procedure?

Cease to think about the matter under decision. Cease to feel about it. Put judgment and conscience away. They have had their say. Now let there be SILENCE, for in the vibrant Silence alone is heard the Voice of the Will. The will lives in silences infinitely more potent than our noisy business of living. The machinery of Life is immeasurably more effective in the realm of the will than its counterparts in the realms of mind and emotions. Yet the vibrations in the higher regions are vibrations of stillness and silence. Only in the stillness and the silence can the will speak and be heard. The Voice of the Will is the Voice of the Silence.

Shall I wear this or that? Shall I eat this or that? Shall I enjoy this or that? Shall I say this or that? Shall I go there or elsewhere? Shall I do this or that? Shall I agree to this or to that?

Here may seem to be a number of entirely trivial questions, and to refer them to the will is to seem to make much ado about nothing. But there is no " nothing ", as has already been said. And there is therefore, no " ado ". To consult the will is the most natural course to take, far more natural, far more real, than just to consult the judgment or the conscience. The will's the thing!

But the will must be consulted silently, in calm, unruffled, unprejudiced, silence: in that silence which is without fear, without what we call desire, without the disturbing influence of the lower personal equation, without the restricting influences of time: in that silence which exalts the judgment and conscience of experience and time into the judgment and conscience of that High Purpose which, in the past, has caused us to know triumph and victory, and has victory and triumph in store for us for all time to come.

Its decision may be in conflict with the judgment of the lower courts. And in so far as we have in general trusted to the decisions of the lower courts alone, save at rare intervals, we may feel a little doubtful as to whether, in fact, we are actually hearing a decision of the court of superior judgment, until, perhaps, something seems to flash in upon us as a bolt from the blue. If we can afford to wait a little before acting upon the decision we shall find that the judgment of the higher court becomes more and more insistent as time passes, more and more obviously right. The more we meditate upon the flash which seems to have come to us—the phrase " think about it " is expressly avoided since to think is so often to confuse and make obscure—the more, if indeed it be a flash from the real, shall we grow convinced of its truth. If, on the other hand, it have some other origin, there is likely to be a flickering, a waxing and waning of its apparent worth, which will cause us to feel we do not know where we are. The lower judgment and conscience often have this effect. But a genuine flash from the will—never!

If there be no time to wait, we shall have to depend upon our gauging of the intensity and brilliance of the flash. If it seem to be a lightning-bolt from the blue, the risk of acting on its message should be run. Otherwise, we may feel constrained to be satisfied with the lower judgment and conscience—taking care, as far as we may, that neither are, to use the expressive phrase of a judge in an earlier period of English history, the judgment or conscience of a fool.

But, as a principle, let us have the habit of consulting the will in every little detail of choosing, to bring nearer that time, which must surely come, when the will shall be absolute monarch throughout his dominions, and the mind and emotions his perfect agents.

CHAPTER IX

YOU AND LOVE

THEOSOPHICALLY speaking, Love is the most wonderful power, the most wonderful quality, in the world. The greatest of all powers and qualities is Love.

Love is in fact the purest reflection both of the unity and of the creative power of Life, of God, of Nature. Love is the truest knowledge any individuality, of whatever kingdom of nature, can ever possess of all that life really is, of all that life can and shall be.

Love is the Great Experience, the mystical transcendence of the less, the mystic dwelling on Olympian heights, the splendid merging of time—even if only for a time—in that eternity which sent time forth.

Love creates the world, sustains the world, regenerates the world. Love is the beginning of growth, the way of growth, the end of growth.

Love is the heart of all things, and shines in and through them more and more unto their perfect unfoldment. There is nothing from which love is absent, however ugly, however seemingly debased. There is nothing which love does not glorify. Love is the golden chain which makes all things one. There is no one, nothing, ignorant or devoid of love, be it but the love Life has for him, or it. While the love of man for man may fail, or the love of man for animal, or the love of man for flower or tree or weed or stone or earth, or the love of any one for any other, the love of Life for all never fails. For the love of Life knows no exclusions, is constant to all things, and is present in tenderness even where no love is seen by mortal eyes.

Love is the Law and its fulfilling. Love is Justice. Love is the universal friend, and comforts all according to the changing measures of their needs.

Love is the Real in the unreal, the Light in the darkness, Life in the midst of that shadow of life which we call death.

Love is Life, Happiness, Peace, Confidence, Endurance, Comradeship, Immortality.

Such is Love as Theosophy sees it. Such is the nature of *your* love, however feeble, however poor, however selfish, however narrow. It may be a passionate love, an exacting love, an aggressive love, a bargaining love. It may be a love that comes and goes, flitting from object to object, from person to person, from desire to desire. It may be a coarse love.

Yet amidst all the dross, the vulgar dross, the ignoble dross, the sordid dross, the ugly dross, the coarse dross, there is shining a diamond, however small, of sparkling beauty and infinite promise. It is the diamond of Life's sublime purpose and eternal meaning, and no external circumstances, no ignorance of man, no carelessness of man, no vulgarity of man, can ever dull this diamond of love, though they may indeed hide its light, sometimes even unto a darkness.

Each one of us has experienced this love, somewhere and somehow. It has an infinite variety of permutations and combinations. It is a link between infinitude of objects. It lives where we often think nothing is but death.

If you will look over your life, you will find love in a myriad circumstances. You will find it in love for relatives, in love for some cherished objects of childhood, for some little comrade just your own young age, for some hobby, for a game, for a teacher. You will find it in hero-worship with its changing objectives; in those delightful boy-and-girl comradeships which come and go impermanent, but are indeed eternal while they last; in the adoration you may have had while young for some much older person who happened to be able to kindle your fire, or fan it; in the begining of a love for causes and chivalrous adventurings; in a love, even, for clothes and self-adornment.

And then comes the time for the *grander passions* which also come and go impermanent, yet which, while they last, are never-ending. Hero-worship on a profounder scale will have its place, and admiration for teacher, professor, athletic genius, film-star, actor or actress. Fiery enthusiasm there may also be, for some forlorn hope, for some adventure against a passionately hated injustice or wrong. There may also be a love for the profession whereby you earn your livelihood, for some sport, for some leisure occupation.

And later on marriage, the conception of children, the bringing of them into the world, the guarding and guiding of them in youth, the proud watching of them as they begin to find their feet on the pathway of life, and then a happy-sad losing of them as they find, and go, the way all others have found and have gone. Then a love of memories to add to the love which needs must change, though not diminish, as change its cherished objects.

To all these should now come in its own due time the love of the future, and, is it too much to say, even the love of death itself, at last recognized to be no demon of separation or loss but rather an Angel of the Larger Life. Ignorance forbids such love to most, yet it is one of the most splendid manifestations of love, in which some day we shall rejoice exceedingly. A mighty love indeed is the love of the glorious future, the eager looking forward to it, the impatience for the time when there shall be no more, even seeming, partings, when the lessons of the human world shall have been learned, when you and those near and dear to you shall move onwards together in undisturbable comradeship, and in ever-growing joy. That love, too, has yet to be experienced.

Let us also exalt that beautiful sign of Life's glory, deep and as yet unfathomable mystery, the sacrament of falling in love.

Nothing is more wonderful, indeed, than a falling in love, better were it called a rising in love, even though we may fall out as often as we fall in. While it lasts it is perfection. While it lasts we have never experienced anything like it. While it lasts it lifts us out of time into eternity, out of our smaller selves into an almost unbelievable, and certainly indescribable, infinity. While it lasts it is Divinity come down to earth. While it lasts it is earth ascended into Heaven.

And it matters not that it endures but for an hour, but for a month, but for a year, to be succeeded by despair, devastation, disillusionment, darkness. While it lasts it is eternal, and that is enough.

And what of sex, that sex of which we are so much afraid that we endow it with fearfulness and taboo in order to justify our fear?

What is love, what is sex, what is even sexuality— using this word in its generally accepted meaning— but the instinct in the One of self-preservation and self-realization, and in the individual of becoming more like Life, which is ever creating and reproducing? Is there aught more natural or more necessary than sex?

There is nothing inherently the matter, wrong, with sex or with sexuality. But there is frequently something gravely the matter with them in their expression in these lower worlds. Selfishness is too often the matter with them. Selfishness is the wrong we too often commit in the name of love, in the name of sex. And sexuality, of which none need feel ashamed, becomes an object of shame because it is selfish and sometimes cruel.

The purer the love, the purer the sex, the purer the sexuality, the more it gives, the more it guards and protects, the less it bargains for return, the less is it selfish and grasping. When we love for our small self-satisfactions, when we commit a sexual act because it fulfils a momentary craving, casting away the contributor to our convenience when we cease to have any need, then indeed is love ugly with dross, and we have poured dirt upon the diamond. The act of loving, be it sexual or of any other kind, is one of the greatest sacraments of life, making life holy that it may the sooner become whole. Birth is a sacrament. Puberty is a sacrament. Entry into full citizenship of the Motherland is a sacrament. The engaging in a career for life is a sacrament. Marriage is a sacrament. The conceiving of children is a sacrament. Dying is a sacrament. And other great sacraments there are, known to the faiths of the world. But what greater sacrament than falling in love and the fruits of falling in love? What greater sacrament than the opening of the smaller life to that larger consciousness which is love in its truest meaning and most profound reality?

Is not the most wonderful mystery of life the One becoming the many, and then, out of the many, two becoming one, that once again a One may become a many?

It is the tragedy of today that love has become commonplace, a thing of little account, a commercial affair of giving and taking, of no giving without the quid pro quo of a return, a small pleasure which may be indulged at convenience, something to giggle about, to be clumsily mysterious about, to enjoy as one enjoys a cigarette, or some article of food, or some sensation of an everyday kind.

It is the tragedy of modern life that the apotheosis of love in marriage is degraded into casualness and into an insignificant incident which we may assume lightly and break lightly. A sanctified Marriage is, perhaps, the holiest act in which any human being can participate. It is a solemn dedication and consecration, prior to a divine creation which is only possible by the intervention of the very Heart of Life. Love invokes. Marriage prepares the way. Life descends. Through marriage we enter the sanctum sanctorum of Life, and therein should be infinitely reverent and abundantly happy. Yet to such a pass has so-called civilization brought us that marriage means little or nothing to most of us. It has become a playground for what is in fact the truest form of immorality, the lack of self-control, of honour, of dignity. Divorce is so easy. It must needs be, when marriage is even easier still. And dare we condemn divorce when we do not honour marriage?

Truly, the sacrament of marriage may exist outside its conventional ceremonial and religious forms. It is not necessary to go through a ceremony in order to be truly and reverently married. Yet the inner sacredness of marriage should surely find reflection in some noble outer recognition and form, in some external observance testifying to our reverence and to our will to live honourably in the new state vouchsafed to us.

We often talk, in other departments of life, of the need for reconstruction, for a new deal, for vital readjustment. Yet nowhere is there greater depression, greater misery, than in the realm of love. If the world had a new deal in love, if our educational systems were seriously to take in hand the education of the young in the true art of loving, depression would soon lift itself from all other fields of living. If our educational systems made education for service their keynote, love would soon return to its rightful place in the lives of men and women. But education has lost, or may be it has not yet found, its soul; and its soullessness is reflected in the ugly forms in which beautiful love is dungeoned.

Let us not be afraid of love, but let us place love in a sacred place and worship it.

Let us not be afraid of falling in and out of love, but let us fall in reverently and fall out gratefully and honourably.

Above all, let us cherish love's fruits as these may follow from actions which, in their results, show that after all we *are* Gods, even though but in the becoming. It is the Divine in us which causes us to be able to do the most marvellous in the world. Let us not fear our divinity, still less run away from it, desert it basely. And let us ever remember that woman is the shrine of that which, in every kingdom of nature, is life's supreme event. She is the appointed guardian of all life as it treads, birth after birth, its pilgrim way; and she is the awakener in man of those noble qualities which it is, in part, his mission and purpose to show forth in kingly splendour.

That women should be treated as they are so often treated in this world of ignorance, that they themselves should often so far forget their womanhood as to prostitute their glories to the pursuit of ugliness, that men should prostitute their own priceless chivalry to cruelty and to horrors far worse than the most terrible circumstances of inquisitions and persecutions: all these condemn us as still infinitely far from even reasonably civilized living, and no less far from an understanding of the true nature of love.

Yet love still dwells in our hearts, and reigns as best it can. Poor in dominion, indeed; yet never quite dethroned. And this is our certainty for the future amidst the darkness of the present.

Hatred often stalks abroad. Cruelty often seems to go unchecked. Selfishness would appear to be the most closely followed rule of life. The oppression of the weak by the strong seems as if it would never cease. Ugliness rears its head and pours its contemptuous gaze upon the beautiful. War ever threatens. Injustice remains unchecked. Discord flourishes.

Yet love is unconquered because unconquerable. All else shall pass away, but never love.

CHAPTER X

YOU AND DEATH

" How wonderful is Death,
    Death and his brother Sleep."

––––––

THEOSOPHY has much to say that is extraordinarily helpful when we come to the subject of death.

In the minds of most, death is Public Enemy No. 1, though in rare cases he is seen in his true nature as the Deliverer. Most people are afraid of death, not because they know all about him, but because they know practically nothing about him. Often the process of dying seems painful, perhaps agonizing. And then what happens when the process of dying is complete? Annihilation? Final severance from all whom we love? Some vague condition of consciousness of a spiritual kind the exact nature of which is a mystery that neither religion nor philosophy satisfactorily solves?

In fact, death seems to involve a radical and, from the point of view of most of us on this side of death, a catastrophic change. Living, we feel we know where we are. Dying or dead, we feel we are at the mercy of relentless and ruthless forces of which we know and can know nothing, forces which draw us away from conditions which normally give us some sense of security, leaving us to face an unknown, no description of which, whether in religion, or in philosophy, or in spiritualism, carries any general conviction. And there is always the possibility that there is nothing to describe. For some unfathomable reason this life may be just this life, without past and without future.

Theosophy's outstanding contribution to this urgent problem of death is to show death to be a friend, and no enemy at all.

Theosophy says that whatever death may seem to do, in fact he takes away nothing that is gold, only that which has become dross. The whole of our conception of death is the result of ignorance. Our mourning, our grief, our consternation that in the prime of life some one is blotted out, our resentment that a little child, "with all before him that life has to offer", has been taken away, perhaps from the most tender surroundings, our orthodoxies as expressed in the phrases "irreparable loss", "overwhelming blow", "cruel separation": all these are but the weeds of ignorance where there should be the flowers of knowledge.

Death releases. Death helps us on our way. Death is the doorway to a newer and larger life, through a period of recreative bliss.

Death shatters no friendship, dissolves no comradeship, breaks no tie, frustrates no purpose. If we have friends, death helps to burn away all that is less in our friendship, and all that is fleeting, and draws it nearer to the time when parting is no longer possible. Death helps us to conquer death.

If there are those who, to us, are still closer than friends, death helps to cement for ever in perfect power and purity the tie we hold so dear.

If, on the other hand, there are those from whom we feel separated by a greater or lesser degree of antipathy, death takes upon himself the role of a great alchemist, and slowly but surely helps so to readjust the situation that gradually the antipathy changes into understanding and goodwill, and finally into friendship, if not more.

Death ever adds. Death ever gives, and his gifts are things of beauty which are literally joys forever. There is indeed only one criticism of death which may be respectfully advanced—respectfully because he is such a benefactor. We must expect to miss the form we have loved, and the physical propinquity which has been a source of constant joy. Surely no religion, no philosophy, not even Theosophy, can quite, at all events at our present stage of evolution, obliterate that sense of aching void when the physical body, and all that the physical body has meant to us for many years of comradeship, disappears. We remain on earth, and automatically send forth actions to which we expect reactions, unable for some time to realize that though we may call there can normally no longer be a physical answer.

The answer of death is clear. He says:

"I grant that you may feel sorry for yourselves when a loved form disappears. I am a little sad for you that, for the very sake of the individual you love so deeply, I must help him to rid himself of a form which hampers his development. But let me assure you that I have come to him for his good, so you must try to be happy for his sake even though you may be sad for your own. And let me now explain to you a little of the process which I know has caused me so much unpopularity, and has made me not a little feared.

" It is, of course, true that your friend's outer covering, which he had to wear in order to meet the rigours and take advantage of the opportunities of the physical plane, no longer exists. But that is all that has gone. Your friend is not only as much alive as ever he was, as much your friend as ever he was, as happy as ever he was: rather is he more alive than ever, more your friend than ever, happier than ever. And he wishes he could make clear to you that your sorrow for yourself is really an extra burden upon him. He feels so free, so much closer to you than ever, so much more full of joy and hope than ever before, that it is by no means an exaggeration to say that he dances round you in all the fervour of a sense of wonderful release.

" And you? You are surrounding yourself with the dark clouds of depression and gloom. You are turned inwards upon yourself. You shut yourself off from his sunshine by your clouds. You may think his departure—it is in fact no departure at all—hard upon yourself. He thinks that your gloom is hard upon him. You say, and perhaps, because of your ignorance, with some justification, that you cannot help it. He replies that you might try to help it, and that one way of trying is to find out what death really does mean."

Ignorance cannot be dispelled in a moment. But the more we know the happier we grow, and Theosophy is in fact the knowledge we need.

Theosophy declares that death helps us out of our outworn clothes, or clothes no longer suitable to our needs, frees us from their restricting effects and thus from all the pain and suffering ill-fitting or worn-out clothes so often involve, renews in us the sense of power so confined when we are in residence in the physical body, helps us onwards to a Heaven in which we find all that gives us real happiness—making life a delight, a source of the keenest anticipation; and finally conducts us back to earth for further sowing and reaping in the fields of the physical plane.

Sleep does some of these things; for when we sleep we also drop the body we use on the physical plane, but then only temporarily. We come back again next morning. When we die we return next life. *Therein lies all the difference.*

Now how are we, in the midst of life, to prepare effectively for death, so that when it comes to us we may be able to take full advantage of it, and when it comes to those near and dear to us, it is as little devastating as possible?

Probably some readers will regard this question as morbid and depressing. They will say that the subject of death is very unpleasant, and that the less we think about death the better.

The subject of death is unpleasant because we think about it wrongly. Every subject is unpleasant about which we think wrongly. We think of death as a destroyer, as an annihilator, as an enemy to ourselves personally, and we think all the more harshly about him because we have the feeling that sooner or later he will be too much for us.

A healthy-minded individual, with a minimum of that ignorance about death which is the cause of so much sorrow, will make friends with death, treat him as a colleague and helper, and give him sensible co-operation when at last he comes. And if ignorance has not been at work year after year erecting what it thinks to be formidable barriers against death, barriers which death so easily overcomes, then not only will death be less inclined to be tiresome, but, when he comes, he will feel at home as with a friend. We tend to summon death the more we seek to repel him. And death must smile to watch the frantic efforts we make to keep alive, when so often he would be able to offer a far more profitable condition than that which we call life, which is but the shadow of a shade of life.

What we have to do is to make death part of our scheme and plan of life. We must give him his due place in life, for he is as much life as that which we call life. He is called death only because he is a different kind of life.

An individual with the necessary foresight might sometimes do well, provided he has also the necessary commonsense and freedom from morbidity, to imagine himself as on a bed of sickness, suffering much pain.

Today in good health, he will hope to exhibit when ill the qualities of patience, endurance, unselfishness, gratitude, and courtesy, especially to those who are looking after him, and generally to all who from time to time come to see him. If he be in fact approaching the need for the services of valet-death, to help him off with his overcoat, he will want to watch without the slightest apprehension the kindly valet drawing near. He will want to calm the grief of those who are fearful—for themselves, let it be realized. He will want the physical body to be as disciplined as possible during the valeting process, so that he may eventually move about in his less restrictive garments easily and without awkwardness. The time will, of course, come when he will be taking off more clothes. But he need not bother about future valeting while the thick overcoat, needed in the somewhat inclement physical plane weather, is being removed for his return to more seasonable climes.

Let him study this business of death as Theosophy so wonderfully and so hearteningly describes it. Let him study the business while he does not happen to be engaged in it. Let him study the technique of it, since sooner or later he will have to observe it as it will be affecting him. Such preparation will immensely help him at the critical moment. And when people wonder that he is so calm about that which is so agitating to most, he will probably reply: " Ah! But I have had the advantage of knowing beforehand what was coming. Forewarned, you know, is forearmed. And I find there is everything to look forward to, everything to gain, AND NOTHING WHATEVER TO LOSE."

Something like the following might well be, as Theosophy would suggest, our general envisagement. Here we are with physical body, feelings and emotions, mind, and some kind of higher consciousness. We are travellers, and we have come to a certain place for business purposes. That place is the world in which for the time being we are living. We must make the best use we can of the place, with all its facilities, opportunities, and disadvantages. But we are careful to plan for a voyage which under no circumstances ends here. Many people do plan for a voyage. But they plan for the present and for the immediate future. They plan as if there were no death at all, or they plan up to death and no further.

But we, enlightened by Theosophy, plan for work and growth far beyond the coming death, and all the deaths which shall succeed this one. Most people hoard themselves in the small stockings of the present and the immediate future. We, on the contrary, invest ourselves in the Bank of Life, which knows no death nor limit of time. We make the best use we can of what we are and of what we have. But we plan so that that which cannot possibly be achieved in this life shall nevertheless occupy us even now, to the end that some day our dreams, our visions, our aspirations, our ideals, may, because they are true, become real and actual. Death thus becomes no obstacle, but definitely a help.

We say to ourselves: Well, we will get this and that done this life. We will try to accomplish such and such. But if we cannot achieve all we plan for this particular life, there is plenty more time before us.

We will go as far as we can in this life, and then death will step in and prepare us for going further in the next. It does not matter that we fail. There is only a limited amount of time available, and we must just do the best we can in it. There need be no cause for regret that we have been unable to achieve all we had hoped. What cannot be done in today's life may be achieved in tomorrow's life, or in the day after tomorrow's life, or in a later life still. A life is but a day, and there are many days.

All sense of helplessness and hopelessness entirely disappears. No student of Theosophy who has learned to apply the Science to himself would ever feel discouragement, or sense of failure or of impotence. "What I cannot do today, I shall accomplish some day. I cannot expect to be able to do everything all at once. Things which could be done in so short a space of time and so easily would hardly be worth doing at all."

So the wise individual not only works at things which he expects to complete in this particular life, but also even begins things which will require attention during many lives ahead. He will want, perhaps, to become a great musician, a great artist, a great scientist, a great philosopher, a great statesman, a great orator, a great writer, a great religious teacher, a great benefactor of mankind, a great soldier or sailor, a great merchant. As for this present life, such hopes must be but dreams; but if he understands the nature of death rightly he will begin even now to lay the foundations for climbing to the heights he longs to reach. Being sure of the future, he will sow seeds in the present for the harvesting of those fruits for which he is happy to wait, sure that the harvest follows the seed.

How different life would be if we planned right across death into the new life and beyond.

How delightful it is, as some of us know, to plan what we are going to try to do next life, what we are determined eventually to become, to treat death as a milestone on the way, to feel that we can accomplish whatever we will, to know that death, far from stopping life altogether, has the contrary effect of speeding it up.

How delightful it is, as some of us know, to realize that the frustrations by which we feel ourselves hedged in, our ailments, our misfortunes, our incapacities, cannot last very long, that the tiredness we feel, especially as we grow old, will entirely disappear under the friendly ministrations of death, that death is a rejuvenator, and that we shall enter upon the next life with all the *joie de vivre* with which most of us entered upon this.

Though death may come, from time to time, to shake us out of all the various relationships which we treasure so clutchingly, thus making us resentful of what seems to be a curse, the fact is that death comes merely to disturb us out of relationships which are less beautiful and eternal than they are designed and destined to be, in order to exchange them for relationships with the same, and indeed a growing, band of comrades, but of a quality ever more and more closely approximating to reality and, therefore, to beauty.

It is rather hard on death that he should be so shunned as he moves throughout the world on his mission of blessing, yet in that dreadful disguise of a curse in which our ignorance has enclosed him.

Yet he remains the tender friend, for he is one of Life Eternal's greatest and truest Messengers, and perhaps it is time that some of us should know him and see him for what he is.

Death has in fact so few, if any, terrors for the Theosophist that the idea of preparation for death while in perfectly sound health seems not only natural but prudent and far-sighted.

One or two considerations may now be added here. First, the physical body having a definite and independent physical existence apart from the individual himself, often resists death even when the individual who is no less concerned is heartily acquiescent. Often, an individual for whom death has no terrors finds that death *has* terrors for his body, and feels apologetic for the nuisance the body is making of itself. The struggles and agonies we sometimes see at deathbeds, the obvious reluctance to die, are as often as not the disinclination of the physical body itself for disintegration—perhaps quite natural, since the physical body does disappear. It has had its day and ceases to be; but it would fain have had a somewhat longer day.

The individual himself is generally quite ready to go, because he knows there is nothing terrible about death, and that he is in fact not only leaving a prison for a garden, but is not losing a single happiness which he has experienced on earth—except those

sense-gratifications which are no real happiness at all.
Friendship, affection, comradeship—all survive death,
as he so clearly perceives; though he deeply, but sometimes impatiently, sympathizes with those round about
him who have not that vision which approaching
release confers upon him.

It is, therefore, important, while control is easier,
to insist upon the body being the good servant it is
intended to be, and not the dictator which in fact
it so often is. While health is good, but specially
when health is somewhat indifferent, it is worth while,
as an investment, to discipline the body, refusing it
the satisfactions it often craves, so that it may gain
the habit of due subservience while the individual
himself is in a position to enforce it.

Then, when death approaches, the body will be the
more likely to remain the servant, and not run riot
when control grows weak. The very intention of
the hitherto ruling individual, which will always be
to prohibit the body from making a fuss and a fool
of itself, will be enough, to make the body mind its
" p's " and " q's ". But if we are accustomed to
give in to the body, then willy nilly it will make an
exhibition of itself on the threshold of disintegration,
the more so if we have been living largely in terms
of the physical body and its lower desires.

This brings us to the second consideration.

When the physical body ceases to exist we are left
without a medium for the satisfaction of those desires
which are connected largely with the physical body.
We are no longer able to satisfy appetites which in a
measure demand a physical body for their complete

fulfilment. We are no longer able to satisfy the demand for appetising food and drink, for the physical element in sexual gratification, for the soothing pipe or cigar or cigarette, for the stupefying drug, or for any other lust connected with the physical body. Inevitably there arises in what is left of us the sense of an aching void, and if we are foolish we shall make desperate efforts to fill the vacuum, obviously without success.

It is well worth while to make the after-death life infinitely easier by gradually reducing the physical aspect of living, without, of course, in any way injuring health. The older we grow the more we should leave off habits which require the physical body for their satisfaction. Then, when the time comes to die, the body will be far less coarse, and we shall not have to take with us a number of enslaving desires which will very truly give us hell, or at least purgatory, on the other side of death.

Sometimes, when Theosophists advocate these sensible preparations for the new life which succeeds death, they are called kill-joys, because they advocate discrimination between the pleasures that give nothing but pleasure and the pleasures which sooner or later will be found to give pain. Of course, if an individual says he does not care about the future, and that he wants to enjoy his " pleasures " while he may, he is at perfect liberty so to do. But while he may thus be physical plane wise—he is not so in fact—he is most certainly other plane foolish.

Theosophists try to be prudent people, and think it silly to live carelessly when, by a little wisdom, the whole of life might be made far happier than is possible under the dominance of the short-sighted view. Nothing which stops short at any particular plane can be really satisfying. Quite apart from the physical body, a life which is largely centred in the feelings and emotions will give us much trouble when the time comes for the emotional body to be dropped as, earlier, the physical body has been dropped. We shall then be similarly haunted by the lower emotional cravings which there is no emotional body to satisfy. No less will a life largely circumscribed by the lower mind give us trouble when we finally shed that particular body to go to Heaven in the higher regions of the mind plane. Pride, coldness of attitude, hard and narrow thoughts of all kinds, separative thoughts —all these will distract us when we would fain cease from distraction, and are eager to take refuge in the higher mental regions in the midst of aspirations and great dreamings.

All these cravings will have to work themselves out on their respective planes, run themselves to death, before we can pass onwards. They must needs keep us back by their insistence and down-dragging propensities.

Let us take death happily and foresightedly into account before the actual process begins to intrude itself upon our notice, as we can well do if we are students of Theosophy.

Incidentally, we should be busy about our attachments to those near and dear to us. Their bodies may be precious, and we shall surely feel pangs at the passing of these. But their souls, that which in each of them is eternal, should be more precious still. And if, through the body, we can perceive the eternal soul, and become its comrade far more than just the comrade of the body, we shall reduce to a minimum the agony of the physical loss. We shall see these persons, who are so near and dear, as age-old comrades whom we have ever had as fellow-travellers, and who will travel with us onwards until for us all the sting of death shall cease.

In other words, let us constantly be adjusting ourselves to the eternal and to the real, so that no outer circumstance, be it death or any other change, can ever make us feel that we are losing hold on immortality, or colour with shrinking fear our thoughts and feelings with regard to an inevitable which is supremely glorious.

CHAPTER XI

YOU AND A MODE OF TRANSCENDENCE

THE author feels no apology is due for the insertion of the chapter which follows, for while it deals less with " You " and with your everyday life, yet it is on a subject which should be very near and dear to all hearts. This chapter expresses the author's personal understanding of music as illumined by the major truths of the science of Theosophy. The word Theosophy is hardly mentioned. But every sentence breathes the very soul of Theosophy *as he understands it*. This chapter is, therefore, an example of Theosophy at work in the author's kingdom of music. In the kingdom of music of another, Theosophy will probably sing a different song. For the author, Theosophy has glorified music and made it intimate. In this chapter he has tried to put into words something of an illumination which, after all, is for him personally. If, therefore, the chapter be dull to read, let it be remembered that it was delightful to write, however feeble the result may be. May the reader who feels disposed to stop at the first paragraph remember that he has his own music within him, and in the light of Theosophy he too may be moved to try to give some expression to its awakened surgings.

The writer of this book is a musician. He is also
an artist. So is every reader of it. Therefore should
there be for each a musical and many other modes
of transcending the less, however different from
the transcendence described hereafter. Hence this
chapter.

There is no fact more important in life than that the
whole of the evolutionary process, and every individuality constituting it, is one vast song, one vast symphony, beginning on a theme dating back to the in-
finitudes before our evolutionary process was born.
Whence the theme? Let a little story be told about the
theme and its origin.

In the infinite past there was a spark of life, one
among a myriad multitudes of its fellows, which
started on a great journey of unfoldment. Because it
was a spark it wanted to become a flame, and then to
become a fire. For it somehow knew the nature of its
Progenitor, and that like must become like. The
Progenitor sent it forth, as He sent forth its myriad
multitudes of fellows, with the blessing: " Go thou
and become likewise! " And the Great Progenitor
aroused in the spark a wonderful note of music, as
also a wonderful tone of colour, which is another
story. It seemed to be but a single, simple note. Yet
enfolded within its simple singleness lay hid a
potential song of exquisite complexity and marvellous
grandeur, embodying in cascading richness a very
wealth of sound. This song was in truth a perfect
echo in wondrous uniqueness and yet in fascinating
difference of the Divine Song in which the Great
Progenitor made vocal His own nature and offered

homage to the Cosmic Father of His Being. And the note of music was the Song in embryo.

The spark was a son of the Great Progenitor, and must needs partake of His Father's nature.

So was the spark sent forth, or rather so was he stirred to awake, to arise, to seek and to find, the mighty Song that some day should be his, his very Self, so that in his own turn he might make his nature vocal and offer the glorious homage of perfection to Him Who sent him forth. Already a sound vibrant with latent but perfect musical unfoldment, he found himself becoming gradually aware of a world of music without him; and its waves beat ceaselessly upon his own slowly-stirring self. Perchance, too, as from a far distance, vague intimations whispered to him, as yet undiscerning, of what seemed to be but a riot of sound-gorgeousness. And impotently he reached out after this vagueness as a baby reaches out after the moon, but some day to grasp, as some day a moon is grasped.

So began he his adventure in music, as also in colour, and today he is the mighty Progenitor of us all. As He was awakened and unfolded to His Divinity, so has He awakened us that we too may become Divine.

Thus each one of us set forth, each with the gift of his own individual note, and with the promise of his own individual song to voice with ever-increasing glory his everlasting life.

The Song of our Father who lives in His Heaven of Sound is singing in the lives of every living thing, and is sung variously as are the innumerable differences constituting the orchestra of rock and stone and earth, of river and stream and sea, of grass and flower and tree, of creeping and crawling and jumping creatures, of every type of human being from savage to saint and genius, and of those who dwell in kingdoms mightily beyond.

Take away a single note, a single song echoing, in its beauty, the past, and hinting, in its unfinished melody, the future, and the great Conductor has lost an instrument precious to Him and essential to His work. So is it that all life is immortal.

In the mineral kingdom the little note hears from all the mineral life around him the call to know his sound and to make of it a song. Thunder, lightning, earthquake, avalanche, storm, trickle of smallest rivulet, torrent of mightiest falls, stillness of deep lake, calm eternalness of mighty mountain and age-old rock, movelessness of plain and unruffled sea: all these are life singing of life's splendour and inconceivable majesty, are life singing the song of its own eternity.

And those who have the ears to hear, may hear.

Hearing these through ages of singing, and himself joining in the song as a child joins in a choir of children, at last he knows the song by heart, and sings it in the song of the diamond, in the song of the sapphire, in the song of the emerald, in the song of the opal, in the songs of the kings of the mineral world.

And those who have the ears to hear, may hear the song of his triumph.

So singing his song of achievement, he passes upwards and begins to learn the song of the vegetable kingdom.

Every blade of grass, every leaf of tree and shrub, every seed, every bud and flower, every tree and branch, is singing its own individual song, and the little note which is now just a fragment more than a note, for his sound has become stronger and his hidden music is faintly sounding from within, is stirring to a music which it has not yet known, but which he recognizes to be of his very nature and eternal rhythm.

And the sound goes forth in forms of fragrance, of perfume, of colour, singing all the while in the terms of a life thus far on its way.

The little note hears and hears; hears and at last learns. Then in his own different way he adds his own distinction to that song of the vegetable life which each member of the kingdom is interpreting according to his own uniqueness, as in fact each member of the mineral kingdom in his own individual uniqueness is interpreting the song of the mineral life.

Thus is kingship in the vegetable world achieved, and a kingly tree, a kingly flower, sings forth the kingship which has been attained.

And those who have the ears to hear, may hear.

Thus is differentiation at work. Thus the varying types, almost bewildering in their variety, begin to voice the sounds and songs specific to their different natures. The diamond nature draws near to diamond comrade. The emerald nature draws near to emerald comrade. The opal nature draws near to opal comrade. And in the vegetable kingdom flower-type, tree-type, draws near to flower comrade and tree comrade, and all sing the song rising from the common note which each shares, though differently.

Each little band moves onwards, perhaps together, singing its type song, chanting the WORD which was in the beginning, which was *with* God, for it was more than God, and which *is* God, for it is the utterance of His Life and Being.

And those who have the ears to hear, may hear the song of triumph.

In stately tree and glorious flower a life in the vegetable kingdom attains his kingship and sings, in all his glory, the victory song of the vegetable kingdom. Then he enters the lowly levels of the animal kingdom to learn his song in still fuller richness—not another song, but a melody, a variation, on the original theme, which has not yet been heard. In the animal kingdom is to be heard the song of the mineral life and the song of the vegetable life. These songs are the background for the *motif* which now in steady crescendo runs through the new kingdom of unfoldment.

In the mineral kingdom we may hear the song of life before it reached even the mineral stage of growth. Those who have ears to hear may listen to life as it grew in its pre-mineral outpouring, may hear the music of its growing. And fulfilling this early music is the mineral *motif* with its variations according to type and difference.

In the vegetable kingdom the mineral *motif* becomes the immediate background, as the pre-mineral *motif* recedes further still and becomes remote, though not ultimate, for only the song of the Great Protagonist

is in any sense ultimate; and even His song is echo of
another Song sung before the beginning of our time.

To these *motifs* is then added the *motif* of life in
the vegetable kingdom, swelling gradually to its
apotheosis. And type selects type once more, draws
near to type-life and to type-form; and the band
moves onwards singing. And now in the foreground
is the *motif* of the animal kingdom, causing vegetable
motif to recede into the immediate background. Kingship in the animal kingdom is reached in noblest
forms. A richer and more splendid song is heard, the
song of triumph proclaiming that yet another stage of
the Great Way has been reached and passed.

Imagine the most beautiful animal you know as just
a song. Cease for a while to see the form, to touch
its deliciousness, to thrill to its joyous vitality and
grace. Try but to listen to the song of its being, a
silent song to those who have yet to hear; to them,
maybe, no song at all; but to those who hear, a veritable song of life, a song which rises to the very
heavens. Hear the song of the life in which it learned
its earliest lessons. Hear, in the very animal himself, the
song of his triumph as a king in the mineral kingdom.
Hear in him his triumph voice declaring to God's
Majesty that yet another of His children has reached
one of the great salvations, hear him summoning Him
who sent him forth to open the door leading to a
salvation beyond. Hear in your loved animal friend
the song the compelling sounds of which shall one
day cause another door to open to his life, that he
may draw near to the final salvation of the lesser
kingdoms.

Surely may you hear in lower kingdoms those other songs which mark ascensions into a heaven whence there shall be ascent to a finer earth. You may hear the songs of mineral life, of vegetable life, singing their way to fuller being. But in the animal who is on the threshold of your own kingdom, who is about to begin to learn to sing the song you yourself are learning, the triumph song of a salvation which gives him kingdom-comradeship with you, must give you special joy, for you know the song, even though differently from the way in which he shall know it. You have sung it yourself, you remember it almost as in an ecstasy, you feel as if once again you were rejoicing in salvation, and you gain fresh courage to move onwards to that salvation in which all lesser fulfilments merge.

Those who have the ears to hear, may hear the songs of savage animals, of civilized animals, and above all of kingly animals.

And now the song of life in the human kingdom is being sung by us all. Earlier *motifs* form an all-penetrating accompaniment or background, through which the original note unfolds still more of that eternal melody which, kingdom after kingdom, has sounded forth in growing volume.

At last we hear this song of life as never have we heard it before. At first we were asleep and heard not. Then we stirred and caught faint sounds. Then intimations of melody fell upon our awakening ears. Then we began to hear a song. Now in the human kingdom we hear ourselves—and those around us. Now in the human kingdom we begin consciously to desire to hear music, and to live lives of music. Heretofore, we have sung unconsciously. Now we have to sing consciously. Now we have to discern our eternal notes, those notes with which we began our pilgrimage of song; and we have to pour into our singing the utmost glory of this human kingdom.

Now have we to sing with all the awakened consciousness of our being, fully realizing the meaning of each note in the melody of our individuality, causing note to follow note as the power and wisdom of individual nature develop.

We have to learn to use the mind to sing truly and nobly, the emotions to sing feelingly, reverently, aspiringly, the body to sing purely: all to sing creatively, so that some day when we have achieved the salvations of the higher kingdoms we may sing the whole Song of our Being in the magic and mysterious calling to an ocean of sleeping life around us to stir to wakefulness and beyond.

At first we say that such and such is music, and that such and such is discord and cacophony. At first we shut our ears to what we think is noise and ugly clamour. At first we judge, applaud, condemn. And one generation will often condemn that which the next generation exalts.

Little by little, however, the song of our own individual eternal meaning and purpose rises above the medley of vocal life around us in every kingdom of nature. At first, more often than not, it rises as a very complex song, full of intriguing permutations and combinations, with shadows of discord and frustration, of failure to resolve. Life seems very complicated, and in our singing we reflect its complexities. Yet, though we sing so complicatedly, and often so discordantly, our song is indeed but an unfinished melody, for it only expresses us as we are in terms of a given time. It is an unfinished melody because neither minds, nor emotions, nor any other consciousnesses, are more than very limited in development. The melody is unfinished because we think we cannot carry it beyond death. The melody is unfinished because we think we cannot carry it beyond the restrictions of faith, race, nation, belief. The melody is unfinished because while to a certain extent the past sings to us, and the present in somewhat greater volume, the future, to our undeveloped hearing, though not in fact, is silent.

Who among us, save indeed some of the greater poets and artists and musicians, and the really great in any other department of life, can hear the music of the future, or the music of the eternal? Who, hearing a scale of notes, will be able to say of one of them: This is my note in so far as the instrument can give it sound? Who, hearing a melody or a sequence of harmonies, will be able to say: Such sequence of melody, such development in harmony, describes the essence of my own being? Who, hearing the singing by some great personage of his own song of life, will be able to say: Such a song as to its glory I shall some day sing, though of course I shall sing it differently?

We have been singing from time immemorial, but have we yet begun to *hear* ourselves sing, so as to begin to know exactly whence we have come, where we are, and whither we are wending our way? In the

human kingdom we must attain a certain perfection
of hearing, though we are not expected to acquire
perfection of singing. And from the complexities
with which we tend to begin we must move towards
those simplicities of song which are the very foundations of our being, so that, reaching inwards to our
eternal note, we may perceive and appraise the
partial structure which has so far been raised upon
it with the help of the sound-material we have
accumulated in kingdom after kingdom. Thus are
we able to proceed with the construction of some
part of the fine superstructure, the material for which
we gather in this human kingdom of ours.

Nothing is yet real music to us in which we are
still unable to perceive an eternal and basic sound,
in which we are still unable to perceive a purposeful
motif, in which we are still unable to perceive movement to a noble end, or an intimation of a music
for which we have not yet a medium of transmission.

We are not really living unless the music of our
own lives is thus more or less characterized. But
the music of the great, the music of the Gods, and
the music of Nature in all her many aspects—these
remind us we can make our own music sublime.

Let us listen, then, to the music of growth, to the
music of triumph and salvation, to the music of our
future. Each of these music sings round about us,
and in us, everywhere and always.

Those who have ears to hear may listen and learn to
compose themselves in glorious waves of sound, to the
Glory of the Great Composer and Divine Conductor
of the Orchestra of Life, and to their own perfecting.

Whither shall your music—mineral, vegetable, animal, human—lead you? To the song of the saint who fulfils his Life in meditation, mystic contemplation, ecstasy, union with God? To the song of the scientist who fulfils his Life in discovery, analysis, synthesis, Law, Order, Purpose, in accurate presentation of experience? To the song of the hero who fulfils his Life in noble action, fearless adventure, fine chivalry? To the song of the artist who fulfils his Life in the exaltation of form as soul, in terms of exquisite line, of colour, of sound? To the song of the ruler who fulfils his Life in compelling leadership, in great statesmanship? To the song of the merchant who fulfils his Life in righteous accumulation of wealth and in its right distribution, in conjuring from mother earth her treasures for the nurturing of her children of all kingdoms of nature? To the song of him who fulfils his Life in service of whatever kind required and possible for him to perform, whether humble or great?

What shall be the nature of uniqueness of your own song of triumph, the song of your salvation in the human kingdom, calling for the opening of that door through which you shall pass into the kingdom beyond? You have sung songs of salvation before, and at each singing you have ascended from a lesser to a nobler citizenship of Life. Once again shall you sing the song of salvation appropriate to the human kingdom, so that you may pass from human kingship to a superhuman citizenship, and thence again to pass as king to a still greater height.

Can you not hear within you, in your primordial note, at first hidden beyond all hearing but now

substantially unfolded, at least the whisperings of the
song of your eternal and unique being? Are you not
at last beginning to know your song, be it but vaguely?
Then try to sing it in your life, even though your
song must needs, at first, be halting, a distorted and
discordant shadow of its reality. Let the song of
your triumph already begin to sound forth its clarion
call, to proclaim the coming kingship of a soul nearing
the human goal, and, thus proclaiming, to stir its
brother souls to move more eagerly onwards to their
own salvations.

There is an almost infinite variety of sound, all of
it music on its way, sound growing, evolving unfolding. There is the music of the crowd, sometimes
harsh, sometimes sinister and destructive; sometimes
fine and ennobling; generally not a little discordant.

There is the music of an audience at a meeting, to
the measure that the speaker is not merely an utterer
of words, but rather a conductor who conjures and
compels music from those whom he addresses. It may
be the music of appreciation, or the music of disap-
proval, or the music of violent antagonism, or ths
music of reverent following, or the music of critical
consideration.

There is the music of a city teeming with evolving
and conflicting life. Often may its music be heard
more clearly at a little distance.

There is the music of the village, of the church or
temple, of the theatre or picture house, of the dwelling
place, of relationship, of houses, of clothes and domestic
appurtenances, of ships, of business, of machinery, of
children playing and at work, of trains and aeroplanes, of

mighty engineering works, of pictures and sculpture, of books, newspapers, magazines, of the very food we eat.

There is emotional music, mind music, physical music, music belonging to every state of consciousness, music expressive of every phase of thought, every changing feeling, desire, hope. There is the music of despair and hopelessness, of sorrow, of joy and laughter.

It is all music in truth, though at our level of evolution we may fail to perceive it as music, so full does it sometimes seem to be of what we call discord.

Discord is but music in the becoming, but so-called darkness gradually resolving itself into light. And sometimes discord is music fallen asleep.

Try to follow your favourite musical artist or composer in his or her own explorations into those regions in which the true artist makes his discoveries, be these in terms of sound or colour or some other mode of form.

Every great artist contacts his glimpse of the oversoul in some state of veritable ecstasy, in some state in which he is lifted from the normal into a supernormal condition of consciousness. He may be an artist in words, or in some material substance, or in any other medium through which life finds expression. In every case he reaches a higher region of consciousness, in it responds to some fine vibration, either simple or complex, then returns with a memory which he proceeds to express and elaborate in a marvellous creation, or, as it really is, in a reflection of the more unfolded life, thus giving birth to an intimation of the larger consciousness.

In the case of some creative geniuses, the vision
which at length is brought to earth is perceived in a
basic simplicity, in a single note vibrant with over-
tones, in a single line infinitely suggestive, it may be,
of implications, in a single colour rich in potential
development. As the vision recedes from its own
plane and descends to earth, the simplicity unfolds,
until at last it emerges as symphony, as statue, as
painting.

In other cases of creative genius the vision begins
in greater complexity, and may descend to earth losing
some of its splendour, rather than in a condition of
unfoldment.

In all cases, of course, there must needs be some
kind of loss as the medium of expression becomes
more dense. The very unfoldment itself is a loss from
one point of view. And often will the seer be sad
that he is utterly unable to reproduce his vision as he
saw it, as it thrilled him. In reproduction, it falls
almost unforgivably short of its reality.

Try, when you are listening to music, to understand
its spiritual or more eternal meaning and teaching,
for music may be a scripture no less than a book, as
indeed may a painting, a statue, a building. A bible
may be in words, but it may also be in colour and in
sound. It surely is so in nature, in the sunrise and
the sunset, in the landscape and in the ocean, in the
stars and in the clouds, in the songs of birds, of
torrents, in the winds, in the rustling of trees, in the
humming of insects, in cataclysms, in storms, in the
stillness. Lose yourself as the music leads you towards
your larger self. Lose the lower regions and dwell

awhile in the higher, thus readjusting yourself to your real self. Most of us are far too taut in the gripping of our lower and lesser selves. We clutch them so desperately that we become their slaves. Music is one of the most potent forms of release from such slavery, provided it is the higher music and not the lower. The lower types of music are doubtless music, for where is music non-existent? But they are forms of music which should have receded well into the background of our being. To force it into the foreground is to cause us to reproduce in ourselves a period of evolution which the civilized among us should long ago have passed. What is the use of repeating a lesson we already know? Why go back to the earlier classes in the human school when we should be near to the close of our school career?

It is of paramount importance that we should not only listen to music but also ourselves create music. In the west little encouragement is given to creative activity in the realm of music, and far too much stress is laid on appreciation of music already composed. Yet from the earliest period of musical study the urge to create should be strongly stimulated. However crude the early attempts may be, it is of very great importance that the young musician—and we are all musicians—should be at work discovering music, playing about in music, experimenting in music, seeking his own note and his own song. Just to teach a child scales and general technique, and to reproduce the composition of another, is hardly teaching music at all. For really to teach music is to help him to enter first into the life and soul of music, and only afterwards to direct his attention to its forms. First must he love music, then should he try to make a little music of his own, and then seek to reproduce the creation of a master musician. We only truly appreciate a magnificent creation when we have already some idea of what it is to create. And in course of time an increasing appreciation of masterpieces should lead us to realize that we ourselves are masterpieces of music in the becoming, and so stir us to reproduce ourselves in sound, just as we might no less reproduce ourselves in colour or in some other mode of form.

The music of India, while without the harmonies which characterize the music of the west, has a great advantage over its western counterpart in that it stresses musical composition with extraordinary success. At every Indian concert part of the programme will consist in improvisation on the part of the various performers. The singer will improvise, and the violinist will actually accompany the singer in a most marvellous way. The violinist will then improvise. And then the wonderful Indian drummer will improvise on the drum alone, giving a startling exhibition of the power and music of pure rhythm.

In few western classical concerts might we expect to hear improvisations by a singer, violinist, a violincellist, an oboe player, a flutist, or by the magician who plays the drums. Yet improvisation and composition are far more vital to true musical art than reproduction. There should not be a single individual unable to do something in the way of musical composition. An individual who declares he is no musician, no artist, no painter, is not telling the truth. He is supremely each one of these, though he may not have the power to express them in recognizable terms. Each one of us is a musician, an artist, in his heart, and surely sometimes sees and hears himself in sound or colour terms. He may not be able to play or to paint, but verily has he in spirit made beautiful music, painted a glowing picture, conceived a glorious form.

With the aid of Theosophy, its inspiration and pure impersonal revealing of eternal truth, the creative faculty becomes finely stimulated. Thus do we draw nearer to our Divinity of which the very soul is the spirit of creation.

CHAPTER XII

YOU AND THE QUEST OF BEAUTY

Is there any outstanding and general use to which we can put the essential principles of Theosophy as we understand them? Is there any service each one of us should render to our surroundings because of the Theosophical understanding of Life we may possess?

Obviously, the work of every true Theosophist, be he a member of The Theosophical Society or not,[1] is to render ignorance less potent for ill and knowledge more potent for good. The supreme purpose of Theosophy is surely to dispel, under the power of its light-bringing rays, those dark clouds of ignorance which so effectively obstruct and distort the light each living creature needs on the way it has to tread. Each individual, in the human kingdom at all events, should be steadily growing aware of the little he really knows, of how much more he is bolstered up by belief, by hope, by authority, than he is strengthened by experience. He should be gaining an increasingly clear conception as to the limitations of real knowledge, should be growing more and more eager to transcend such limitations, and to venture forth beyond those frontiers which are conventionally accepted as impassable.

[1] Anyone is a Theosophist who lives according to Theosophical ideals.

Theosophy not only gives each one of us a clearer perception of the nature of the knowledge we really possess, but also intimates to us in no uncertain language the nature of that wisdom which lies both on the threshold of and far beyond our present ken. Hence, with the help of Theosophy, we are not only able to set in order the house of our present knowledge, but also to prepare plans for that larger and more commodious dwelling which sooner or later we shall be anxious to build to house the more we are beginning to desire to achieve.

There are, of course, innumerable directions from which to enter upon a clarification of the knowledge we possess, and so to lay foundations for the larger knowledge beyond. But it would be helpful to know of the existence of some general principle common to all directions, part of the eternal and universal foundation of truth, whatsoever forms it may take.

If such a general principle exist it would be useful to strengthen it where it already holds, and to give expression to it where it is, so far, absent.

One such principle, at all events, seems to me to be the principle or quality of Beauty, inherent in all that is true, in all wisdom, in all power that is spiritual in its nature. Theosophy, declares that only the beautiful is essentially true, shows the beautiful to be the supreme heritage of growth, demonstrates the beautiful to be the enduring fragrance of experience, and foreshadows the beautiful as an increasingly dominant factor in the lives of all who live naturally and therefore truly. And surely is it obvious that in the world today ugliness has no small dominion, at the expense of Beauty, and therefore at the expense of Peace, Goodwill and Happiness. There should be more of the beautiful in the life of a Theosophist, whether or not a member of The Theosophical Society, than in the lives of most ordinary individuals, for Theosophy is the Science of Beauty because it is the Science of Truth. The smallest details of his daily life should, therefore, have a touch of beauty uncommon in their nature. He should be living a more beautiful life, with more beautiful feelings, more beautiful thoughts, more beautiful speech and action, more beautiful hopes, aspirations and relationships with his fellow-men.

He should be able to perceive the beautiful in all around him more clearly and more appreciatively. His relationship with nature must be a more beautiful relationship, because there is more of beauty in him to make contact with the beauty without. Nowhere is beauty entirely absent. We may be unable or perceive it. It may exist but in embryo. It may be hidden underneath much which does not conform to the particular standard of beauty it should display, to that beauty which is natural to it. But it can never be said that anywhere beauty is non-existent, for beauty is of the essence of life, and life is universal.

A Theosophist, if he be well versed in his science, should be sensitive to beauty in no matter what form of life. Most people might insist that in certain forms of life there is no beauty at all, that it is overflowing with ugliness. But the Theosophist knows that however full of so-called ugliness a form may be, it is eternally redeemed by a spark of beauty, however feebly the spark may glow.

What, then, is ugliness? Does it exist at all? Is ugliness prevalent in the world today?

Will the author be understood if he defines ugliness either as beauty out of place, as that which for an earlier stage of evolution might have been beauty, but which has ceased to be the beauty appropriate to the later stage of evolution; or as undeveloped beauty, beauty at a primitive stage of unfoldment. Ugliness is often beauty in the becoming, and no less often beauty out-of-date, is a form or some other mode of consciousness from which life should have already withdrawn to enter forms more closely approximating to higher development. Ugliness and Beauty are, therefore, relative terms. It might almost be said that some modern artists have reproduced for the evolution of today the beauty of thousands of years ago. This beauty is no longer able to perform for us the duties of the beautiful, and therefore we term it, or should term it, ugly.

Ugliness, therefore, often exists because we do not release ourselves in time from that less which once may have been beautiful for us, but which now is ugly because we are holding fast to it when the time has come for us to let it go. Ugliness is prevalent in the world today both because we are not yet so very far on our evolutionary way, and because the world might well, but does not, ascend more rapidly from the rung of the evolutionary ladder on which it at present stands towards that rung on which it should be standing even now, or is destined to stand tomorrow.

There is much that is beautiful in each one of us. There is much that is beautiful in all the world. But there might be more. There is to be more. There might be more wisdom. Then would there be more beauty. There might be more brotherhood. Then would there be more beauty. There might be more reverence and understanding. Then would there be more beauty.

Is it possible, then, to give a general definition of the beauty of which each one of us, and the whole world, stands in need?

Yes and No. Yes, in the sense that civilization has reached a certain level which demands for its true expression certain specific reflection of Beauty. There is a Greatest Common Measure of Beauty for the world of today as a whole, for the world which is calling itself civilized.

No, in the sense that each individual has and needs a beauty peculiar, unique, to himself.

The beautiful which X should display, towards which he should strive, may well be a beauty radically, though not fundamentally, different from the beauty appropriate to Y.

A savage, for example, has a standard of beauty which in the more civilized individual might quite accurately be described ugliness, because the civilized man should have finished with the use of that particular kind of beauty.

The standard of beauty for an animal, and for each kind of animal, will be different from the standard of beauty generally appropriate to the human kingdom. Similarly, with regard to the vegetable and mineral kingdoms.

And the standard of beauty appropriate to a super-human kingdom will surely be radically different from that which suffices for the human kingdom.

Beauty and ugliness, therefore, are, as I have said, relative terms. The ugly is generally the outworn. The beautiful is that which as perfectly as possible expresses the individual at his actual stage of evolution, both as he is and also, in intimation, as he is to be. But the moment he begins to be ready to pass from the less at which he is, to the more which awaits him, that which has been beautiful will begin to become " ugly " for him in so far as he is unwilling for it to become absorbed in the new standard of beauty natural to the larger life on the threshold of which he stands.

Everything in all life is beautiful, for everything has its place in life. But it is beautiful in its place. Out of place it appears, and relatively is, ugly. The beautiful is that which is in its place, and the beautiful for us is that which helps to bring us into most beautiful and uplifting harmony with our particular stage of evolution, expressing us at our best and truest, and helping to move us forward on our way. The beautiful not thus helpful and expressive is not beautiful for us where we are, is not *right* for us, though we have to learn to appreciate its beauty *where it is right*. And the beautiful at a place higher than that at which we are is not yet beautiful for us, though we have to learn to begin to appreciate its beauty *where it is right*. We must on no account despise beauty which has helped us to attain our present stature. Its beauty, where it is, remains, even though we no longer have need of it. Nor must we remain content in the beauty for the moment appropriate to us. This beauty, too, must in its turn give way to nobler beauty still, which as soon as possible we should be striving to understand and embody.

We must humbly yet ruthlessly, in homage to the life in us which should be a river flowing with ever-increasing power and purity, examine the veriest details of our daily lives, as much in their intimacies as in their larger aspects, to be sure that we are expressing the utmost beauty attainable by us where we are.

Are there uglinesses in our homes, in our tastes, in our desires, in our attitudes, in our speech, in our actions? This is to say, are we living below the standard natural to us at our present stage of evolution?

Let us look at our clothes. Let us look at our living rooms. Let us look at our food. Let us look at our work. Let us look at the quality of our power of appreciation. Let us look at our leisure. Let us look at our opinions and convictions. Let us look at our hopes and fears. Let us look at our relationships.

Are all these as beautiful as we are able to have them? An artist might go into our house and condemn it as irretrievably ugly. For him it might indeed be ugly. But the question is whether it is ugly for us where we are. An individual with highly developed taste as regards dress might judge us to be more than dowdy and crude in our attire. Are we more dowdy and crude than we ought to be—where *we* are, not where he is?

An individual highly sensitive as regards food might condemn our meals as impossible to eat. Still, they may be right for us where we are. An individual highly refined as regards his quality of appreciation might well turn with abhorrence from that which will delight us. But is our appreciation, though crude for him, as beautiful for us as we can make it?

There is, it would seem clear, a standard below which we should not permit forms to fall. There are surely certain right conventions as to the distinction between the beautiful and the ugly, between that which will help us onwards and that which must keep us back. And we have the duty, through public opinion and individual exhortation and judgment, to condemn the ugly and to insist on the beautiful. We have the duty to supply to the public that which the public needs, not by any means always that which it ignorantly demands, the food which will help it to grow, be this food physical, emotional or mental.

We must set and maintain a high standard of right, and therefore suitably beautiful, living in every department of our complicated lives.

But at the same time we must not imagine that the individual who does not, or cannot, conform to the normal standard has, therefore, no beauty in him. He probably has in him all the beauty available to him at his particular stage of unfoldment, though he may possibly have less than he ought to have. Or, indeed, he may have unevennesses of beauty and so-called ugliness. We must judge each individual, in so far as we have any duty of judgment at all, according to his stature. But we must never think

that in him is no beauty at all, especially if we ourselves are engaged in developing, and probably with
not a little fanaticism, some particular aspects of
beauty which happen to have caught our individual
fancies.

" How beautiful is such and such an idea! How
beautiful is such and such a principle! How beautiful
is such and such an activity! Why cannot people see
how beautiful these are, and abandon the correspond-
ing uglinesses? Why cannot people be as fascinated
as we are by the ideas which to us are so obviously
marvellous and beautiful? "

We must not seek to impose upon others those
beauties which may be natural and right for ourselves.
We must not imagine that because they do not
accept our own particular standards of beauty therefore
they are devoid of the beauty sense.

That which is essentially true for each one of us
is the beauty each one of us must seek to display.
Beauty grows as life grows. Beauty grows as intelligence grows. Beauty grows as the emotions grow.
And as life unfolds in the higher regions it is the
law of nature that between beauty and ugliness the
pendulum of experience and understanding shall swing
with increasing violence, until the intimate knowledge
of darkness awakens in us a perfect appreciation of
light.

In the earlier kingdoms of nature beauty seems to
be more manifest, more apparent. In the mineral
kingdom the beauty of structure, the splendour of
immensity either in terms of mass or in terms of
distance, the latent omnipotence of rushing power,

the glow of fructifying life, the sublime motherhood of matter—all inspire to wonder and to a sense of the space which is indeed beyond our understanding.

In the vegetable kingdom the beauty of form, the glory of colour, the richness of profusion, the silent dignity of the more kindly members of the kingdom— all declare the beauty of nature as the quality of all qualities.

In the animal kingdom the beauty whereby need is fulfilled in form, the all-pervading sanctity and sacrifice of motherhood, the nobility of death as it comes in the fulness of time—all declare the sublime purpose of nature.

In each kingdom, beauty in its crystal-clear simplicity and directness. In each kingdom, beauty in its delicacy and refinement.

No other witnesses are needed to the divinity, design and growing triumph of Life than these young kingdoms of nature.

Life asleep in the mineral kingdom, beautiful in sleep because of the all-perfect Motherhood of That which we call Providence.

Life dreaming and vaguely stirring in the vegetable kingdom, beautiful in dream and stirring because of the all-perfect Motherhood of Providence. Life growing wakeful in the animal kingdom, beautiful in early wakefulness because of the all-perfect Motherhood of Providence.

How marvellously she watches over her younger children!

And her older children—we of the human kingdom? Have we not to learn to become Providences unto ourselves? Are we not to grow into the fulness of the measure of the very stature of a Providence?

In the lower kingdoms protection, and all the unbroken beauty which such protection ensures. So that we often think nature more beautiful in animal, in vegetable, in mineral, especially in the kingship life attains in these, than in the human realm supposed to tower above them all.

Yet in the human kingdom each individual life has the supreme glory of taking his unfoldment into his own hands in increasing fulness. And with that glory comes in due course a vision of the kingship appertaining to the kingdom to which he now belongs.

In the human kingdom, life awake, learning to be free and a law unto itself. And in this kingdom, therefore, the all-perfect Motherhood of Providence helps us to learn to stand on our own feet, not to be led as children, but to move freely as men, and at last to begin to *know*.

Who can know Life who does not know death? Who can know Light who does not know darkness? Who can know Wisdom who does not know ignorance? Who can know Beauty who does not know ugliness? So, in the human kingdom, we can speak the word " ugliness ", and we can know its meaning. And sometimes, while we still do not know, we confer upon the words " beauty " and " ugliness " and their significance to us the quality of absoluteness and finality. We judge, as if for ever.

But when we begin to know, then we learn that beauty reigns through the realms of life, that everywhere she has her dwelling-place and her due reverence.

It must be confessed with sadness that as we learn to swing in growing confidence the pendulum of increasing power, our earlier movements not infrequently cause havoc and desolation in kingdoms of nature which should be sacrosanct from abuse.

To what barbarities are often subject the young lives working their way through mineral, vegetable and animal kingdoms. Well may we learn our lessons upon our kind, but need the pendulum swing so violently that it bruises life it should never touch?

Theosophy proclaims the sanctity of all life, and its rightful inviolability from wanton defamation and destruction. It is time today that the pendulum should swing, moving away its centre as it swings, from the ugliness of the sense of irresponsible possession, to the beauty of the sense of protective compassion. To use must be to serve. To abuse is to injure both subject and object.

Let us seek the more beautiful in ourselves, in our surroundings, in our work, in our leisure and play, in our relationships with life in its many forms around us. Let us be dissatisfied with the beauty we know and appreciate, and wander in search of beauty as yet beyond our power to recognize. Let us know with all our hearts and will that there *is* a nobler beauty to take the place of almost everything which is at present beautiful in our lives.

We can, and someday shall, live more beautifully in the little things of life. We can, and some day shall, be more beautiful in all we think and feel and do and say and like and love.

Ugly living, of whatever nature and wherever existing, is the negation of Theosophy and the frustration of Theosophical living.

Theosophical living means striving to live to the measure of one's highest and ceaselessly seeking to ascend to the heights beyond.

What is an essential antithesis to ugliness? Simplicity. Peace and happiness in simple yet comfortable living, in living which makes no unjust demands upon those who have to toil in industry, in living close to Mother Earth and in constant communion with her, in living far away from noise and evil competition, in living in friendship with all, in so living that desires find their satisfactions in simple pleasures which vulgarize none and degrade none in their making. Indeed is it true that the more closely we live to Mother Earth the farther away are we from all that to us is ugliness.

We often find people imagining and aggressively declaring that the truest simplicity for human beings lies in nudity because there is no clothing for the sub-human kingdoms, lies in eating raw food because animals do not in their natural state eat cooked food, lies in disregarding the ordinary sanctions of human civilization because these sanctions do not appear to exist in other kingdoms.

We often find people imagining that simplicity lies in being as unlike other people, ordinary people, as possible, thus shocking them by that which they must needs regard as extravagant. Simplicity is thus thought to dwell in unconventionality, in the bizarre, in the startling, in the unusual.

But such simplicity is no real simplicity at all. It is little more than an emerging from one rut of behaviour to enter another, a worship of the idol of difference at all costs.

There may be simple living in a hut. There may be simple living in a palace. The millionaire may be living no less simply than the working man, as we use the term, though in truth we should all be working men.

He who is able to find his wealth no less within himself than without is living simply, because he is dependent upon no external satisfaction, and is at peace in his centre, be the contents of his circle what they may.

Ugliness lies in extravagance, in effect for effect's sake, in the exaltation of that which tends to enslave, in emphasizing self-seeking instead of service, in flattering and exalting the body at the expense of the soul.

Each of these types of ugliness can be found, for example, in modern art. There is a vogue, a cult, of ugliness, and the spirit of slavishness is so strong in us that we often feel we ought to be able to appreciate that which is in truth ugly, which we know in our hearts to be ugly, but which people with well-known names declare to be beautiful. It is a sorry spectacle to watch the slaves of the orthodox making pitiable efforts to distort their vision so as to be able to see that which is not there. If only they would trust others a little less and themselves a little more, they might kill that ugliness of form and of colour which is able to raise its head only because so many of us are cowards before aggressiveness.

Let us hasten the day of dissatisfaction with the beauty which for the time being suffices. Let us hasten the day when we shall constantly be seeking the beauty of the future to take the place, in our waking consciousness, of the beauty which serves us in the present. Let us hasten the day when we cease to conjure up, from the recesses of the subconscious, that beauty beyond the qualities of which we have long since grown. In these days there is a very dangerous tendency to revert to the past instead of living forward into the future. We resurrect the circumstances of our savage living, and because they are unfamiliar, unusual, strange, intriguing, we think we are moving forward when in fact we are moving backward. We are moving. Pride will not allow us to imagine we are receding. Therefore we must be advancing. Thus the whole tone of the world becomes lowered to a level from which in truth it has risen; and the result is a coarsening of the texture of life which finds parts of its expression in life's present uglinesses, in the depression, in the constant menace of war, in the unrest which has daily reflection in the press. We are living below our actual worth. We are living below our capacity to live. We are substituting the less beautiful for the beautiful which awaits us, and we are not pressing forward to the more beautiful which is our present heritage.

Let us seek to fulfil the beautiful in ourselves, that which is the beautiful for us at our present level of growth. Let us live in every detail of our lives as beautifully as we know how. Let us beware of electrifying with a cold and artificial resuscitation the worn-out forms of beauty which have had their day, and in garbs of ugliness protest again their outraging. Let us, in the spirit of the beauty which is ours, move onwards to the beauty which shall be ours. Let the beauty of yesterday, of the many yesterdays, sleep the sleep of the just. Let the beauty of today be magnificently awake. Let the beauty of tomorrow already be shining softly in our East.

CHAPTER XIII

YOU, THEOSOPHY, AND THE SOCIETY

IT is of the highest importance to realize that Theosophy is in no way dictatorial. It does not lay down the law, or any law. It does not require an individual to subscribe to any principles, on the ground that their acceptance is essential for right living.

Theosophy is not authority. It is a statement as to the nature of the Science of Life, and only a partial statement at that. You may call it, if you like, a revelation, for it primarily comes from Those who are wiser than humanity. It largely represents that which humanity has yet to begin to learn. But the revelation does not claim to be a Word which must be believed if salvation is to be achieved. It is a picture. And those who look upon it are obviously free to like or to dislike either any part or, for the matter of that, the whole.

If Theosophy is concerned at all with God, it is concerned with the God within each individual rather than with any extraneous God, anthropomorphic in appearance as every such God must necessarily be. Yet Theosophy knows God in a nature indescribable to man. By no means is Theosophy Godless, for the

God-Principle is one of the most wonderful and universal facts of Life.

Theosophy scientifically and impersonally describes, as far as description is possible, the nature of the evolutionary process in which we all live and move and have our being. It describes the past. It explains the present. It draws a picture of the future. And it leaves each one of us entirely free to make use of so much of the description as suits us, leaving alone that which at present has for us no meaning.

Theosophy does not say: Thou shalt. Theosophy does not say: Thou shalt not. Theosophy says: Look. Consider. Weigh. Determine.

A member of The Theosophical Society is in general sympathy with The Society's Three Objects. He is in general sympathy with the principle of universal brotherhood. He is in general sympathy with the desirability of studying the great religions, philosophies and sciences of the world in a spirit of understanding comparison. He is in general sympathy with the idea that there is infinitely more to be known about life than is so far known, and that a venturing forth in search of knowledge is highly desirable.

But his mode of expressing such sympathy is very much his own business, and his way of living is his own concern.

People have very erroneous conceptions as to what it is that characterizes a member of the Theosophical Society.

Many think that membership means the giving up of the religion one has for some other forms of belief, either anti-religious or religious in some other way.

Many think that one must become a vegetarian, a non-smoker and an abstainer from alcohol, in order to qualify for membership.

Many think that members of The Theosophical Society are all pacifists, and would be conscientious objectors were there to be war.

Many think that no one can become a member of The Society who is not prepared to accept some form of authority, a Master, some particular individual as a World Teacher, some unusual form of a religion, such as, for example, the Liberal Catholic Church with respect to Christianity, or the Bharata Samaj with respect to Hinduism.

Many think that members of The Theosophical Society are required to subscribe to some form of political teaching, that they must be opposed to all forms of nationalism, must be exclusively inter- or super-nationalists, that in India, for example, they must all be ardent protagonists of Home Rule.

Many think that The Theosophical Society has specially close affinities with some specific scheme of economic reform, or of humane reform, or with some bizarre and fantastic ideas about ghosts, or about the return of human souls to animal forms, or about psychic phenomena. "Oh! You are a member of The Theosophical Society? How interesting. Do please tell me all about ghosts, and how physical articles may be made to go invisibly from one place to another, and whether you can show me a Mahatma some time. And it is true that you believe we may become animals again? And do you really believe in rein-carnation?"

A member of The Theosophical Society is often regarded as a freak, and sometimes, it must be admitted, with justification. Far from being a freak, however, he is, or should be, a trifle more sensible than most people in the world around him, because he has a scientific conception of life which stands all common-sense test as to reasonableness. Science may not be able to say that its physical experimentations substantiate every detail of the Theosophical picture. Religion may not be able to place its hallmark upon much that Theosophy declares to be true. Philosophy may have no experience to offer comparable with the vistas disclosed by Theosophy. The ordinary everyday individual, leading the ordinary everyday conventional life, may be quite unable to fit into his *vade mecum* what he, and the scientists, and the followers of a religion, and the philosophers, may dismiss as extravagances without the warrant of normal experience.

Yet science, religion, philosophy, and the everyday individual, notwithstanding, a member of The Theosophical Society with his three sympathies, and his own personal understanding of the Theosophical picture of life, has something the world as a whole does not yet possess. It may be little. It may suffer by comparison with some of the grandeurs of the world's discoveries. It may not be susceptible of what is called " proof ", that is to say, it may be unable to find expression in conventional terms, in language and form recognizable to proof-addicts, to satisfy those who regard the mind and its existing frontiers as the final arbiters of truth.

Arraigned at the bar of the narrow present, Theosophy may be condemned, and members of the
Theosophical Society mulcted in the costs of oppro-
brium and ridicule. But at the bar of the future both
will be justified. From the court of the present appeal
ever lies to the court of the future, and not infrequently
the judgments of the earlier court are reversed.

Above all, be it understood that a Theosophist is
free as are few members of the various faiths of the
world. He is free from narrow dogmatism, from
subservience to unreasoning authority, from fearsome
orthodoxy, from everything that is artificial, blind,
savouring of crowds and conventions. He is free
from the restrictions these impose, even though for
one reason or for another he may perchance choose
temporarily to dwell within their restraining circles.

Take any individual member of The Theosophical
Society, and it is impossible to predicate of him anything save a sympathy with brotherhood, a sympathy
with the need to understand and to draw together the
religions of the world, a sympathy with the search for
truth. Is he a member of some creed? Possibly,
possibly not. Is he a vegetarian? Possibly, possibly
not. Is he a non-smoker? Possibly, possibly not. Is
he an abstainer from alcohol? Possibly, possibly not.
Is he a pacifist? Possibly, possibly not.

Does he believe in reincarnation, in the existence of
Masters, in the various teachings known under the
name of Theosophy? Who knows?

The Society is not in the least degree concerned
with any specific ingredients of an individual's outlook
upon life. It is only concerned to ask that he has

three sympathies, not even three objectives which he should be pursuing.

It is the glory of The Society that birds of infinitely divergent plumages flock together in the name of a common brotherhood, live together in a spirit of solidarity, understanding and mutual appreciation, and yet may radically disagree with one another on innumerable apparently vital matters. Each one of us needs other people's differences to make his own more true. In The Theosophical Society differences abound, partly for this very purpose; for in every difference there is truth, even though, blinded by our own differences, we are unable to perceive it.

Some will be vivisectionists, some anti-vivisectionists. Some will be vegetarians, some non-, possibly anti-, vegetarians. Some will be conscientious objectors so far as war is concerned, some may have no such scruples. Some will be ardent followers of this or that Theosophical leader, some may repudiate all idea of leadership and exalt the superiority of abstract principles. Some will be convinced ceremonialists, some no less convinced anti-ceremonialists.

Some will regard the science of Theosophy as the supreme *raison d'être* of The Theosophical Society, some may be no less sure that the advocacy and practice of universal brotherhood, apart altogether from Theosophical teachings, is The Society's sole but entirely adequate justification for existence.

Members of The Theosophical Society are not after one pattern alone, are not cast in a single mould, are not subject to a single creed. God forbid they should be!

Each is free. Yet is each lifted by his membership
into participation in that spirit of solidarity, of real
understanding and friendship, which alone can bring
about peace and happiness.

The object of The Theosophical Society is not mass
production of a single type, but the enrichment of the
whole by the diversities of the many. The Society
welcomes differences, is eager to collect them, is
happy that they should freely express themselves in
all purity and strength. But it does ask that within
The Society at least these differences, however radical,
be pursued with courtesy and graciousness, with
generosity and understanding, and supremely with a
noble recognition of the value to every other member
of the difference which to him is no less dear and true.

Differences matter less. The modes of holding
them matter infinitely. No one is absolutely right.
Everyone is relatively right—relatively to his evolutionary stature and monadic uniqueness. And everyone is in a measure in possession of the "right"
which he needs where he is. Each one of us needs
to be at work making his own individual "right" as
true and as beautiful as he can, conscious that such
is the duty of all.

Membership of The Theosophical Society helps us
in a wonderful way to do this, for in the light of our
membership we begin to perceive that everyone is in
fact shining with his own "rightness", however different from, or apparently antagonistic to, our own
"rightness" it may externally appear.

Thus is it that entry into The Theosophical Society
is entry into freedom, entry into a wonderfully

constructive and heartening comradeship, entry into a world of mutual understanding and adventurous purpose. There are no lines within which the member is constrained to live save those he chooses to draw himself. There is no picture of life he is expected to admire and copy. He is not bidden to worship at any altars, nor to prostrate before any persons, nor even to hold that in Theosophy alone is truth.

He joins a happy band of people who are at last beginning to learn how to live effectively and joyously, how to take all possible advantage of every circumstance that either afflicts or heartens them, to have unbounded yet wise confidence in themselves and their future while adequately conscious of their existing limitations, as also no less of those which may yet have to appear above the horizon of their unfolding lives.

He joins a happy band of people who are beginning to loose all fear, all depression, all sense of despair and of the futility of life, all discouragement, all lasting sorrow, all sense of irretrievable failure.

He joins a happy band of people who are learning to make enthusiasm, courage, truth, adventure and peace dominant qualities in their lives.

In The Theosophical Society there are no inquisitors, no arbiters of spiritual fashions, no dictators, no judges.

The Society is a Society of friendly people, and everyone who wishes to be friendly to all without distinction of creed or class or race or nation, who has no desire, in a spirit of superiority, to impose his own particular convictions upon others, but rather to appreciate them and their convictions, is most heartily welcome to membership.

ENVOI

HERE are the Laws of the Science of Theosophy as I have so far perceived them. They are the Truth within every statement I have made. But other seekers of Truth may see the Laws otherwise. It matters not. What matters is to seek and to find. Each discovery is true within the limitations of the understanding of the seeker. As he grows, the less will become the more. But the truth he has known will never leave him, however inadequate its expression. It has helped him on his way, and is eternally precious.

As the Science of Theosophy, which is the Science of Life, unfolds itself to my gaze, I find that the White Light of its entirety breaks up into the following Rainbow of Principles or Laws:

First—Life, or Consciousness, *Is*. This must be taken as axiomatic.

Second—Life is *One*. One and Indivisible. The One includes the Many. The Many vibrant within the One.

Third—Life is *Everywhere*. I cannot conceive of either a place or a condition with regard to which it could be said that it is lifeless. There may be a minimum of Life, or a maximum of Life, but nowhere a perfect vacuum of Life.

Fourth—Life is *Movement*. I hold that Theosophy declares that Life is nowhere at rest. Life is ever active, moving onward in a ceaseless process of unfoldment. Time is the slow-motion of this process. Eternity is its fulness.

Fifth—Life is *Hierarchical*. Life is ladder-like. On every rung, Life, at one stage or another of progress from unconsciousness to self-consciousness, from slavery to Kingship. Hence the kingdoms of nature. Hence the innumerable differences in each kingdom.

Sixth—Life is *Individuality*. Everywhere, individuality is in process of unfoldment, and becomes more and more marked as evolution proceeds. Even universality is but an expression of unfolded individuality.

Seventh—Life is *Self-Sufficient*. Sufficient unto each individuality are his circumstances. There is no life, in whatever stage of development, which lacks the wherewithal to enable it to move forward. There is no despair, no hopelessness, no blackness, so complete that from it there is no exit. The way out from darkness into light is ever open, *and must be taken*, is ever being taken—even though it may seem not to be taken.

Hence: TRUTH TRIUMPHANT—LOVE OMNIPRESENT—LAW OMNIPOTENT.

INDEX